THE OTHER SIDE OF ELLEN WHITE

PAUL B. RICCHIUTI

TEACH Services, Inc.
P U B L I S H I N G
www.TEACHServices.com • (800) 367-1844

Copyright © 2019 Paul B. Ricchiuti

Copyright © 2019 TEACH Services, Inc.

ISBN-13: 978-1-4796-0927-7(Paperback)

ISBN-13: 978-1-4796-0928-4(ePub)

Library of Congress Control Number: 2019902343

TEACH Services, Inc.

P U B L I S H I N G

www.TEACHServices.com • (800) 367-1844

Author's Note

As I write this book, I am also reading another book that has been classified by the *New York Times* as a best seller. It was published by Crown Publishers of New York.

That book, titled *Quiet*, also has nothing to do with the content matter of what I am writing now. However, I discovered a statement in the beginning of that bestseller that I also wish to incorporate into this volume. I found it to be the desire of both that author and myself to have a clear, uninterrupted approach to easy reading. Therefore, readers will not find many direct quotation marks in either of these works. Thus, in order to keep the reading flow continuous, and free from most source material marks, many of these symbols will be eliminated. They will not be used. Nevertheless, if one wishes further study for research purposes, conformation, and/or verification, the reader will find an available listing of all sources and fact information at the end of this volume.

Dedication

I dedicate this book to Doctor Paul Jansen, who is more than just a friend to me. I consider him as a real son, one that I love dearly. I long for the time when I can be with God: and live with both Jesus and Paul in Heaven.

Table of Contents

Foreword

A large section of this work will be centered on Ellen White's years spent in Australia. Those years, however, are not the main purpose of what I am attempting to achieve. No, my efforts will also take us to other areas of the world beside Australia … areas where this little lady once lived. Thus, my aim is not centered on travel or any one location, but instead on presenting a human being, a woman—a very normal, down-to-earth woman—named Ellen White.

Many people think of this person as not being human like the rest of mankind. However, she had wants, needs, feeling, likes, and dislikes just as everyone else does. She felt pain, disappointment, sorrow, love, anger, compassion, hope, anxiety, even fear. Is that so strange?

This presentation, then, is a portrait of the Ellen White I wish to emphasize, present, describe, introduce, if you will, in word pictures. And I fully believe you will like what you find. At times I will, in reference to certain events, use her formal name, Ellen White. In other instances, I will use her first name only. There is, as you will discover, a definite reason for this.

Here then, is a woman who most people say was different.

And what do I mean by different?

Just this!

When it comes to friendship, Ellen White and God were on a meaningful one-to-one basis. Can you say that about yourself? He wants you to. He asks you to.

But let's face it—she was, shall we say, different. Oh, she had two eyes, ten fingers, two feet, and everything else that goes to make up a human being. But here is the difference. She had a brain that was in tune with God. She saw Him. She talked with Him. She listened when He gave information only He and she shared.

We can't do that.

So what makes the difference? Visions and dreams are a partial answer. She had both. This is the way she and heaven communicated. The Bible is full of examples for this kind of interaction between God and humans. Transfer of messages, between heaven and earth, were not given through things such as news broadcasts, personal views, warnings, or other methods. No, they came direct from heaven by speech, eyesight, dreams, or signs. These methods, through time and ages, involved both men and women.

Ellen White was one of these people.

But now, just for now, shall we put this information on hold in order to have a better look at this one human being? After all, that is what she really was … a real living, breathing, person, and a woman.

I invite you to read on.

Introduction

I have a question. Tell me, who—or what—spoke to, or gave, Ellen White information that made men and women sit up and take notice? What made people listen to her? Why? Was it her personality ... her commanding presence?

No.

Could it have been her education, contacts, or even the authority of her speaking voice that did it?

Again, I say *no*.

Many who saw or heard this woman often trembled or even broke into bitter tears.

So, once again, I ask the question, "Why?"

She knew names, faces, even carefully hidden secrets of people she never saw before or even met. How could this be?

Open your Bible and turn to Second Samuel, chapter 12, and verse 7. This is when God's prophet Nathan pointed to King David and said, "Thou art the man." This story is not new. David had a man named Uriah murdered so he, David, could marry the man's wife, Bathsheba, and Nathan knew it. This man Nathan was, as I said, a prophet.

I personally believe, without question, that Ellen White was also one of God's prophets. God worked through her to pass His messages to people individually, in groups, or to institutions.

In recent years an alarming trend has been growing among some members of the Seventh-day Adventist church. They claim that Adventist preachers quote the works and words of Ellen White more than they do the truth of the Bible. And this should not be.

I agree!

Ellen White would say the same.

I will also add that if this little woman were alive today, she would condemn that practice. She, herself, called her works a lesser light pointing to the greater light: God, and the Bible, His Word.

I fear that many who think this negative way use this trend as an excuse to ease their conscience and leave the church.

Yet, why is this action a surprise? The Bible predicts this would happen in the final days of earth's history. There will be scoffers.

Second Peter 3:3 tells us this. I quote the Revised Standard Version (RSV). "First of all you must understand this, that scoffers will come in the last days with scoffing, following their own passions." Thus the assault on the gift of prophecy comes as a warning. It is to be expected. She, and the Bible, warned that the end of earth's history is near, and that scoffing is one of the signs.

Think about it. If the prophet Nathan had not pointed at King David and had never said, "Thou are the man!" he would not have been God's ambassador in human form. He was authorized as God's messenger. This man was only doing his job when he pointed at David and said what he did.

As a general rule, people are more interested in hearing about gossip and flaws in others. This is usually because they wish to take pressure off themselves and their own actions or beliefs.

Thus, when Ellen White, in Australia, pointed to bickering, disagreements, jealousies, grudges, and other actions in the Adventist publishing house, and other places, what was their reaction?

Did they say, "Pay no attention to her? It is none of her business what we do." This attitude is and always has been one of Satan's most effective and greatest tools. He used it on Eve, and he is doing the same today. Without knowing it, this type of attitude is downgrading the messages God gave, and Who still is giving, through the Bible and a woman named Ellen G. White.

Satan's plan is to take something good, something vital and essential to man, and twist it into his deadly purpose by making it of little or of no value. His tactics and methods of deception are clever. They are no different from those he used in heaven itself. He claimed he could do whatever he pleased. He bragged, "I will be like the most High" (Isaiah 14:14, KJV).

And look what happened.

So, I ask you, who is it that critics are anxious and eager to judge? Is it Ellen White, God, or both?

Ellen, like Nathan, did as God asked her to do. And it wasn't easy. God also told them both it would be rough. And, it was.

When Ellen first stepped foot into the Adventist Publishing House in Australia with her message, she spoke in loving tones. And how did they react to her being there?

We have the answer in her own words. "The brethren," she wrote, "confessed to one another and fell on one another's neck, weeping and asking forgiveness ...."

She and God were successful.

Living the life of a human being is serious business. Think carefully. Be honest with yourself. Serve God, not your earthly self. Then, and only then, will you have a clean, clear mind, and no one can point a finger at you and say, "Thou art the one."

Who was Ellen White anyway? Was she just another human like the rest of us?

Yes, she was.

And as you continue to read on, you will find she also walked hand-in-hand with her best friend God. May we do the same!

So now you have it, my reason for writing this book. It is quite simple. I just want you to become acquainted with a wonderful little lady who, although I have never met her, is one of my best friends.

Most pictures of her show a woman dressed in black, sitting on a chair and looking stern, stuffy, and unfriendly. This is a mistake. She was not that way at all. Ellen White was a warm, caring woman in love. And when someone is in love with another being, such as she was with God, a burst of happiness follows, and it shows. This is the Ellen White I know. Oh yes, she had serious messages to give the world, ones that involve you and me, but that never stopped this delightful woman. She knew happiness, joy, sorrow, heartache, pain, suffering, betrayal, and everything else that you and I know. After all she was a human being. But there was one thing about her that I admire the most. It was her sense of humor. She knew how to laugh, and that took her through many rough places.

Let me explain.

Now, if I have already written the following story in one of my other writings, all I can say is, "So what else is new!" It needs to be told and *retold*.

During the last years of her life, Ellen White lived in her home named Elmshaven in northern California. Elmshaven was a happy place. I visited there many times. It was mostly when her granddaughter, Grace Jacques, lived there. Grace was a delightful little person, full of life and fun, and she was always gracious and loving to everyone. We became friends.

I believe it was Grace herself who told me this story, or maybe it was Arthur, her brother. It doesn't matter, because it is a story I will never forget.

Pacific Union College was, and still is, located near Elmshaven and students often visit that home. While Ellen White was still alive, and lived there, a young man, a student at the college, bragged that he was going to visit Ellen White and maybe, just maybe, have dinner with her. This was an ego trip with him to gain popularity. No one believed him.

In fact they made fun of him, For Sara would never allow it to happen. And who was Sara? She was Ellen's traveling companion and nurse. And no one, absolutely no one, got past Sara to have access to Ellen White. Some called her Ellen White's watch dog.

She knew how to laugh, and that took her through many rough places

One day this young man went to Elmshaven and was immediately met at the door by Sara. "No," she said, "You can't see her." But Sara was no match for this young man. He had a way with women, and he charmed her completely. As a result, Sara opened the door widely and let him in. She then introduced him to Ellen. It was a delightful visit—so great, in fact, that she asked him to stay for dinner. This was exactly what he wanted.

Ellen White was enjoying this. Yet she was wise to him and secretly suspected why he had come. But she said nothing.

There were other guests for dinner that evening, and everything went well until the dessert. It was lemon pie, a favorite of Ellen White's. But something was decidedly wrong. Because when

566

everyone took a bite of the pie they quietly pushed it aside. All of them did this except for the young man. He then became the center of attraction as they watched him almost gag at every bite he took until his portion was gone. He ate it all.

Ellen was watching. And there was a gleam in her eyes. She suspected that something was definitely wrong with the pie. She had not eaten, nor even tasted, her piece.

Looking directly at the young fellow, she smilingly remarked, "I see you like lemon pie."

What could he say but "Yes"? After all he was trying to make a great impression on her. She then added, "Would you like to have my piece? I am too full to eat it."

There were snickers as he slowly said, "Yes."

Finally, as he was struggling to eat the last bite of that second piece of pie, the cook rushed in. "Please," she said, "Don't anyone touch the pie. I used salt instead of sugar."

The place was in an uproar. They were all laughing, including Ellen White, and no one seemed sympathetic toward the young fellow. If he was silly enough to eat two pieces of salt pie, they thought, then, he should suffer the consequences. His face turned red, and when he finally returned to the school, he never bragged about his visit to Elmshaven.

Ellen White did have feelings for the fellow. She liked him, but she also felt sorry for him. He had a problem. And, as mentioned, she suspected what he was doing by coming to Elmshaven. Her inner feelings told her he had a lesson to learn, and she was pleased by the outcome, hoping the lesson had indeed been learned.

This is the Ellen White I have come to know. She was a real, live, delightful human being instead of a finger-pointing institution as some call her.

In researching for this book, I discovered, to my surprise, that Australia seemed to become a turning point in Ellen's life. I believe this hit me when I learned that she and her staff were living in a tent while her home was being built. If you recall, she did not want to go to Australia in the first place. But now, here she was, and she was having a house built. It appeared she planned to stay.

Why? What happened?

I believe the change came because there were very few Seventh-day Adventists in and around that great country. Did this fact trigger something in her memory? People in Australia seemed to possess a pioneer attitude. This was something she had not seen in a long time, and she suddenly realized she missed it.

I have heard, and it has been said, that the earliest days of any institution or new venture are its best days. Was this a reminder of the time when the Adventist church was just getting started? Those were hard, but good, days with no formal organization. People worked together with one purpose in mind—to spread the good news of the Gospel, the seventh-day Sabbath, and Christ's soon return. There was no power struggle (politics) to claim top positions in that organization. And in fact she had, at one time, suggested to church members not to settle in or cluster around the centers or headquarters of the organized church. They were doing just that in the United States, but not in Australia. "Move away," she had said, "Spread the message to both rural and city areas." But very few were listening.

One basis for her thinking comes from a letter written to Doctor Kellogg. She was writing from Elmshaven. The year was 1900. This home was thousands of miles away from the official church headquarters in the eastern part of the United States. In writing about Elmshaven she wrote, "[at Elmshaven I can] keep out of the din of battle."

In another letter to the General conference, also from Elmshaven, she wrote, "Here I am retired from the strife of tongues."

A church paper, *The Review and Herald,* stated her thoughts as she returned to the United States. "I wanted to remain in Australia. I love the people there, and I love the work. I have not lost my love for Australia, nor my interest in the workers there."

The words, "strife of tongues," tell us a great deal. They suggest that she was under stress for much of her life, mostly from church officials. That is one reason for the phrase" ... out of the din of battle," which was definitely having its effect on her.

Now, to bring this subject front and center, let me tell you a story. When I first began working for the Pacific Press in 1955 (and don't ask how old I am), I met a long-time employee who also worked there. We became friends. I asked him if he had been working at the Press during the time of the fire in 1906. He said, "Yes." Then he added, "And I can tell you all about it."

This is his story.

He stated that at the time of the great San Francisco earthquake in 1906, the Pacific Press (a few miles to the south) was heavily damaged. An entire wall fell out at one end of the building. As a result, the workers became discouraged. Many wondered, *Will it be rebuilt? If not, will we lose our jobs, even if it will be rebuilt?* Tension was rising. The management met, and finally decided to ask Ellen White to come from Elmshaven, not too far away, to encourage the workers. Thus, they sent a delegation to her, urging her to come. Her answer was a decided, "No! I won't go." A second delegation was sent with the same result. She said "No," again. Finally, a third and stronger group went to see her. Her answer was "I told you **NO** twice."

Pressing the issue, the committee finally asked her the reason for not wanting to go. She answered that the Press people would not listen to her before, so why would they listen to her now? Why waste her time and theirs? This group didn't give up until she finally gave in and said, "Yes, I will come."

The entire work force assembled the day she came. And they listened to her intently. But in the middle of her message of encouragement she stopped speaking, looked directly at the workers and said (I am paraphrasing), "If you don't stop doing that commercial work in the Lord's house, something worse will happen to you than that earthquake. But when it does come, just remember one thing—the Lord is the best friend you will ever have." Following this statement, she finished her talk and then went back home.

The commercial work continued as the Lord's work was set aside and suffered. But the Press was making money from it, and lots of it. Three months later, after her visit, the entire Press burned to the ground.

The man telling this story to me said that on the night of the fire he was the last person to leave the building. It was around midnight and it was his job to lock up everything. He finally locked the front door and started walking home. Most of the workers lived within walking distance. No one was in the building.

About a block away, something told him to turn around and look. As he did so, he saw that the building was as it always had been, and it was securely locked. But as he continued to look, he saw something unusual. There was a strange light moving around on the roof. There had never been a light up there before, and there should not be one then either. Soundly, as he continued to stare, and all at once, the entire building was wrapped in flames. And it was not just a small fire. Flames leaped everywhere in all parts and sections of the building. Firemen came, but the fire was so fierce they could not contain it, and the entire building burned to the ground. Nothing remained.

The Pacific Press was re-built, and it is still in operation today. The lesson was learned. All commercial work stopped. "The din of battle;" were her words. She and God knew what those words meant.

They knew them well.

Ellen learned to face people as they really were. She did it, and her sometimes harsh treatment to others was because she loved them. And she did it as far away from the center of the church's headquarters as she could. Her faith and love for the church never wavered, however, even though disappointment and disillusionment seemed to follow her every step. This gave her a deep insight into how God must feel toward His fallen creation, mankind.

"If you don't stop doing that commercial work in the Lord's house, something worse will happen to you than that earthquake. But when it does come, just remember one thing—the Lord is the best friend you will ever have."

And that involves every one of us.

I might add that all direct quotations on the pages of this book, including Ellen White's own words, published or spoken, can be verified as true. One prime example is that "strife of tongues" statement of hers. She had endured so much stress and criticism in and around Battle Creek (the center of the Adventist Church) because of her work and role in the church that it began to take its toll on her physically. It showed! But when she moved far away from all of that, she found relief at her new home in California—Elmshaven. It was there that she began to unwind at last and finally relax, thus, her reason for the *tongues* comment. That statement is located in a book written by her grandson, Arthur White. The book's title is *The Early Elmshaven Years,* and the statement appears on page 36. Other such quotations can be found in the listed references of the bibliography at the end of this volume. These works—mostly books—were written for anyone to read, study, and research.

"Surely the Sovereign Lord Does nothing without revealing his plan to his servants the prophets." Amos 3:7, *NIV*

Chapter 1

Far below the equator, stretching toward the South Pole, beyond oceans and such as the China Seas, and south of the Philippine Islands, sits a land of extremes. There are mountains, but not like the mountains in the United States, or Europe. These mountains appear to have been eroded through centuries of time into rounded highlands. The tallest is 7,328-foot Mount Kosciusk, featuring snow for only part of each year. Ancient forests, small lakes, and forbidden deserts are a major part of this unusual place. Rivers and tiny streams usually dry to a trickle or vanish completely in the extreme heat of summer. It has modern up-to-date cities, with the world's latest technology. These centers swarm with people in ever growing numbers. They thrive mostly along coastlines, or in the far south, where temperatures are cooler.

This is Australia.

There is an ongoing debate about Australia. Is it an island or a continent? If it is an island, as some say, because it is surrounded by water, then it would be the largest one on earth. From east to west it measures over 3,000 miles, and from north to south it reaches nearly 2,000 miles. It rivals the United States for size. The Pacific Ocean is to its west, and off the east coast is the Indian Ocean. The total land mass is approximately 2,984,827 square miles. What a great place it is, this island (?) continent (?).

Thursday morning, December 12, 1891, saw the passenger liner Alameda steam into Sydney harbor and drop anchor. Among its passengers were a group of seven Americans. They were up early that day to see the harbor, said to be among the most beautiful in the world. Before going ashore, they lined a deck, leaning against the ship's railing, and searched the wharf and the waiting crowd below. Suddenly a cry went up, "I see them!" was the shout. "There's

Elder Daniells and Mary!" spoke a woman named Ellen. She waved. Shouts came back, and when the gangplank was finally in place all were soon together on shore and talking at once.

The trip had been a long one. It began in San Francisco on Thursday, November 12. There were rough seas and ports of call such as Honolulu, Samoa, and New Zealand. Crowds met the ship at each stop, anxious to see and meet a passenger named Ellen White. At Samoa, natives met the ocean liner in canoes and small boats, selling fresh pineapples, bananas, oranges, mangoes, limes, and coconuts. They also had shells, coral, mats, baskets, and fans. All these were made from local grasses. It was a colorful, happy event, a spectacle filled with sunshine and laughter.

But Ellen White was not there.

So, where was she?

Writing!

She was in her stateroom writing. Ellen was in the midst of creating some of her most important books, on the life of Christ. When the news first came, by invitation, that she was needed down under, in Australia, her thoughts and reactions were written down in her diary. She wrote, "This morning," August 5, "my mind is anxious and troubled in regard to my duty. Can it be the will of God that I go to Australia? ..."

She didn't know.

On April 1, 1874, Ellen White was given an unusual vision. An angel she called "The young man," stated, "Your house is the world." He went on to add, "The message will go in power to all parts of the world." Next, he named several different countries. Later, James, her husband, asked her to name the countries the angel mentioned in that vision. She answered, "Yes, I remember one, the angel said Australia."

As a point of interest I would like to depart from our subject for a moment to relate a conversation I had with Arthur White, Ellen White's grandson. I was at the White Estate near Washington D. C. doing research for a book on Ellen White. Arthur, in charge of the estate at the time, and I had become friends through my contacts with him at the estate. As we talked, on one of my visits, I asked Arthur this question. "What did the angel look like that came to

Ellen White during her visions." Without hesitation he described that being in detail. He also added that this information had not been written down; instead it come through members of the White family as told to them by Ellen herself. This is what he said.

"The angel was tall, had a handsome face, a well formed, athletic body, a warm smile, and was dressed in neat, clean, contemporary clothes. In other words, there was no bright light, no wings, only a young, fine looking man, dressed in the ordinary clothes of the day. He looked and acted like everyone else."

I did not believe what Arthur told me.

A few years later Arthur came to visit me in my office at the Pacific Press. While there I asked him that very same question again. And, without hesitation, he repeated the exact same answer.

This time, I believed him.

Now back to our story.

A puzzling question raises itself concerning that ocean voyage. It would take her halfway around the world. She knew that all too well. But in her heart she longed to stay in the United States. Thus, before the trip, she was tom between two options—to go, or to stay. She also felt God wanted her to make that long voyage. Everything pointed to it.

And instead of sightseeing, she planned on producing several hundreds of pages of writing while at sea. This was a main reason why she remained in her stateroom at Samoa instead of going ashore with the rest of her group. She was trying to write.

"I have not been able to do much writing on this voyage," she wrote. "I have written about one hundred and fifty pages, but I expected to write as much as three hundred pages ... I was almost completely exhausted in mind and body when I came on board the vessel."

Ellen's reference to being exhausted in body goes back a few years. In Colorado she had a hard fall. Both ankles were broken. In re-setting them, the attending doctor re-set them wrong. This made her a partial cripple for the rest of her life. Now, on that voyage, she depended heavily on assistance while walking, especially in rough weather. This drained her strength.

She was also dreading something else. It was, but, let her tell it herself. "I am not so sanguine [naive] enough to take an optimistic view of events or conditions or to expect favorable outcomes in regard to this [her messages to the Australian people from God] .... They know nothing of me and my work personally, only through my writings. Reproof is unpleasant to the natural heart, and the reproof coming to the people as I know it will come to them with opposition. Already envy and evil surmisings and jealousies are at work ... There is want of spiritual knowledge ... to discern the work that needs to be done as the Lord shall open the way."

With this in mind, is it any wonder why Ellen hesitated on going to Australia? But she went anyway, and each word she wrote, every sentence, all paragraphs, and every page her pen produced, was a love letter. And people who read her writings soon learned that Ellen White was deeply in love with someone and she did her best to tell the entire world about the affair, and who it was she was in love with. It was none other than God Himself.

So, why was it that Ellen went to Australia when she really didn't want to go? She felt she had good, solid reasons not to go? There was even a clause in the invitation from the General Conference. It stated that the decision was hers to make, and hers alone. Oh, but the stubbornness and determination ... she had both those qualities all right. And she knew how to use them. And she could stick by them if and when she didn't want to do something. So why then did she decide to go to Australia, and where did she get her energy and drive to do so?

One answer comes from verse 50 of Psalm 119. It reads, in the Living Bible, as follows: "They [God's promises] give me strength in all my troubles, how they refresh and revive me!" She and God were on a first name basis. And whenever He asked her to do something, she did it without question. She, being human, may have had doubts, but she did as He asked anyway. He wanted her to go to Australia, and made it possible for her to do so. It was as simple as that. And she went!

Thus, knowing that God was with her regardless of whatever awaited, such as possible resentment, misunderstanding, or even jealousy itself, she went! It would not be an easy experience, and she expected it.

Sidney was a fine, modern city in the 1890s, and it remains the same today. It is located on the southeast coast of that gigantic land with its magnificent harbor. 1891 saw a well-organized, cultured city. Stately mansions dotted its hills, all facing the sea. Private yachts filled its harbor. Parks surrounded public buildings. The Town Hall, with its giant clock tower, was a masterpiece of stone and cement-like lacework, known as gingerbread. That one building alone, and there were others, was decorated with statuary, spires, tall pillars, iron gates, and a grand entrance.

All spoke of wealth.

Yet forty miles inland, west of the city, is a massive jungle of trees, tangled growth, underbrush, and waterfalls which remains practically untouched to this day. Some refer to it as the rainforest of the Blue Mountains. It consists of over two million acres, under government protection as a natural treasure of parks and reserves. Charles Darwin, the noted evolutionist, was closely linked to this area.

Ellen White's American party of seven did not stay long in this alluring city. It lasted for only a few days. Their destination was Melbourne, a city along the south coast. That city too was a center of activity. It was a seat of learning with a university in its midst. Large impressive buildings also lined its streets and avenues. One, the public library was massive and very impressive.

From a book titled *Illustrated, the Book of The World's Great Nations,* page 663, published by the Werner Company in 1893, we read a description of the city library. "The building is a massive and imposing structure. The lower story is a museum of paintings and sculptures. There are halls filled with busts and sculptures, including casts from the most celebrated specimens of ancient and modem art.

> *With this in mind, is it any wonder why Ellen hesitated on going to Australia? But she went anyway, and each word she wrote, every sentence, all paragraphs, and every page her pen produced, was a love letter*

One hall contains an interesting collection of portraits of Australian and New Zealand governors, and a collection of Chinese curiosities for Melbourne has an important Chinese quarter. On the same floor is a large picture gallery containing many good works. A grand flight of stairs leads to the upper story, occupied by the magnificent free library of Melbourne.

"This spacious reading room is 230 feet long by 50 feet wide and 34 feet high. The library contains nearly 109,000 books .... During the year 1879 the number of readers were 266,839 .... Any man or woman who is decently attired and can behave respectably can have books, shelter, warmth, chair, table, and light up to ten at night, day after day, night after night, year after year, and everything is entirely free."

A side note gives this information, "There are one or two side rooms specially reserved for the use of ladies."

This is the world Ellen White stepped into.

Chapter 2

Before leaving Sydney, Ellen White spoke to members of the Adventist church in that city. Their reaction was instant. They were spellbound. They were amazed, and hung on to her every word. Salvation and reasons for what they believed in were so plain. It drew them close to heaven and one another. Some felt that as she spoke, God Himself must have been standing beside her giving her every word she uttered.

They wanted more.

And did this affect her personally?

From a private letter she wrote, "I am not sorry that I am here." Her feelings of uncertainty were fast melting away. She knew now where she belonged, and she was convinced it was spelled A-u-s-t-r-a-l-i-a.

Why then, didn't she stay in Sydney? And what was her reason for traveling on to Melbourne, her final destination?

The answer is simple. In all of Australia, Tasmania, New Zeeland, and on many smaller islands, the entire Adventist population totaled around 700 members. And Melbourne was the center for the denomination. The conference headquarters, plus the publishing house, were both located there. This made that city the center of the church's activities.

One of the first things she did was to talk with the leading Adventist workers and members of the church. On Christmas Eve she spoke to the assembled group about the full, and real, meaning of Christmas. She mentioned the tradition of gift giving. She said it was a good thing to do. But, she added, those gifts should have real meaning and value, not mere trinkets to waste money on.

One example for what she meant by the term "meaningful gifts" can be explained through the gifts the wise men gave in Bethlehem. These became the means that made it possible for Mary and Joseph to escape with Jesus into Egypt. This saved His life.

> *Ellen began her work the moment she arrived in Melbourne*

Ellen began her work the moment she arrived in Melbourne. I say this because when she entered the publishing house, and walked into the pressroom, she said she had seen that room in vision. She recognized a number of the workers and knew what problems they faced. She also knew there was a lack of unity and harmony. This fact alone made her more convinced that God had led her to the right place.

Satan knew this also. Her weakened ankles were evidence of that. He made it happen to her. Thus, by this action he had looked to the future and made plans to destroy, not only her, but the work God gave her to do. And now that she was in Australia he brought out more of his deadly weapons. Sickness is one of his most effective tools. And he knew how to use it.

Confusion is another of his sinister methods. He applied it to her by confusing her about going to Australia. God wanted her to make the trip, but Satan also knew that God is also not a dictator. He would not force her to go. It was her decision, and hers alone.

Ellen White's grandson, Arthur White, in his book titled *The Australian Years,* page 24, he quoted an entry from Ellen's diary. She had just arrived in Melbourne.

"I was not well" she wrote, "December 26 and December 27 [Sabbath and Sunday]. I had strong symptoms of malaria. I could eat but little through the day and had quite a fever, but the Lord strengthened me when [I was] before the people."

Arthur White made a comment about these words in her diary. He said, "She little realized the ominous [harmful] nature of the situation, for this was the onset [start] of a prolonged and painful illness that was to affect her ministry in Australia ...."

Ellen was not exempt from problems or trials. She knew who she trusted and believed in, and that made all the difference. God and

His will, whatever the case might be, she would, without questioning, obey. His will was always first in her heart and mind.

Almost from the moment of her arrival in Australia, Ellen was struck down with sickness. She wrote, "During this period I experienced the most terrible suffering of my whole life. I was unable to lift my feet from the floor without suffering great pain."

Doctors told her she may never walk again.

At another time she stated, "I am unable to move hands or limbs without pain." And as for her writing, she went on to add, "My arms are so painful, the writing I have done for the last few months has been in constant suffering."

And on top of this, she was thrust into a maddening round of meetings, talks, advising, and counseling, in a land she did not know, and with people who spoke and acted in ways new to her. Then, to add to her misery, she had no place to live. House hunting became a time-consuming drudgery. It was hard work, with very little result.

Yet, in spite of all this, she continued to write. She forced herself to do so. She made the comment that at times she was so exhausted she fell asleep while writing. In a letter to Dr. Kellogg she began to analyze her situation more fully. She did it by talking with herself in that letter to him. "Why do you feel almost forsaken, and discouraged?" she asked herself, "Is not this the enemy's work?" I said, "I believe it is. I dried my tears as quickly as possible and said, 'It is enough; ... And I am happy in my affliction; I can trust my heavenly Father'"

There is a further statement in another letter from this most remarkable woman. It reveals the inner workings of a profound, calculating mind, as she examined and explored her situation with reason. In simple words she stated, "I am now writing on the life of Christ ... It may be I am a cripple in order to do this work so long neglected."

Also, from a manuscript marked 19, dated 1892, she reported, following a group prayer, and an anointing for her recovery, words that were given directly to her from God. He said, "I am your Redeemer; I will heal you."

John 16:24 is a promise she also claimed. "Ask and ye shall receive."

She asked, she believed, and at the right time—she was healed.

Chapter 3

Why was Ellen White so extremely powerful, both in and out of the Adventist church? She had the ability to create fear or reverence. How? Why? Prophets of old like Daniel, Moses, Ezekiel, Jeremiah, and others had this same skill. When she spoke, people listened. Some did not want to hear what she had to say, but they listened anyway. They seemed compelled to do so. Was it, as she claimed, her direct connection with Heaven?

I say "Yes."

To explain my reasoning, we have an example by a man named Faulkhead. The story is somewhat familiar, but not well known.

N. D. Faulkhead was the appointed treasurer for the Adventist publishing house in Australia. He was tall, full of energy, pleasant, yet he also had an ego, a highly overrated opinion of himself. Before joining the Seventh-day Adventist Church he had, and still held, top positions in several important secret societies of the Masonic Lodge. Ellen White knew this when she first arrived in Australia and wrote to the Faulkheads concerning their situation. Her message to them was fifty pages long. She sealed them and was just about to mail the package when, in her own words, she wrote, "It seemed that a voice spoke to me saying, 'Not yet. Not yet, they will not receive your testimony.'" She had already addressed the package of fifty pages to both Mr. and Mrs. Faulkhead. But she didn't mail them.

A year later, Mr. Faulkhead had an unusual dream. In it he dreamt that the Lord had shown Ellen White his connections and dealings with the Freemasons. A few days before his dream, Faulkhead made a remark to a question as to what his reaction would be if Ellen White had a direct message from God about his activities? He said, "It would have to be mighty strong."

Now, Ellen White sent a message that she wanted to see him.

He went.

He arrived just as she was returning from a long trip, and she was exhausted. So she asked him to return the following day. And yes, she did have a message for him from the Lord.

His reply was, "Why not give me the message now?" Without saying another word, she walked to a table, picked up a bundle of papers and said they were for him. She then added that she had planned to send them to him several times but was forbidden to do so. And that was the reason she did not send them. Then she added that the timing was not right for him to accept them until now.

They began talking, and as they did, she described lodge meetings he attended and even to the place where he was sitting. She also saw him giving small amounts of money in church offerings while giving larger amounts to the lodges. And most of all, she saw and heard him being addressed as "Worshipful Master." She pled with him to cut all connections with the Freemasons, adding that if he did not, he would lose his soul. Faulkhead's face turned pale.

She warned him that it was impossible for anyone to be a Freemason and a complete Christian at the same time. Upon saying this she unknowingly made a second sign with her hand

Instantly, after saying this to him, she made a strange hand movement, a sign. Faulkhead was shocked and asked if she knew what she had just done. Surprised, she replied she had no idea what he was talking about. He blurted out that she had just given the hand sign of a Knight Templar.

She warned him that it was impossible for anyone to be a Freemason and a complete Christian at the same time. Upon saying this she unknowingly made a second sign with her hand. Blood drained from Faulkhead's face. She had made a secret sign that was known only to the highest order of Masons. That sign was not known by women, and it was secretly guarded in private meetings, and against strangers, both inside and outside the place they met.

Tears rolled down the man's face as he managed to mumble these words, "I accept every word. All of it belongs to me." Sobbing he said, "I accept the light the Lord has sent me through you." He immediately acted on his decision. He resigned from five lodges he belonged to. He even had control of three of them by doing all their business.

He said later to Ellen White, "I am so glad you did not send me that testimony (the fifty pages), for then it would not have helped me."

Thus, we have an example of how God worked through this woman. There is no other explanation for her actions. This was God's doings through the work, help, and connection she had with Him through an angel He sent to aid her. She had no idea she made those signs until she was told she did them.

This then, is a sample of the reasons why people listened to her. She and God were that close.

In relating the events in the story of N. D. Faulkhead, we learned how God works through the aid of angels. But He doesn't always do this, for sometimes God prefers to perform His will directly. In this instance, however, and unaware of her actions, He chose an angel to show the secret signs to Faulkhead through the action of Ellen White.

This brings up the subject of angels and how they interact with human beings. In chapter one you read about a conversation I had with Arthur White concerning angels. If you recall, I asked what they looked like, especially the one who came to Ellen White in vision, and also in visible form.

So let's talk about angels and their interaction with human beings for a minute. Then we will return once again to Ellen White, a woman in love with God.

From time to time I have been asked, by various groups, to present stories to children and or adults. This, I consider to be a talent God has given me. I consider it as a loan. It is not my doing. I use this method of presenting God to young, and/or, mature minds, and I am more than willing to partner with Him in this venture. I also assure my listeners that God is the best friend they, or anyone, can or ever will have.

I was invited to tell a story to a group of children in a small, private grade school. The children would be assembled, all fifty or more of them, in one room. I almost said "No."

I knew the school's location—or, at least I thought I knew it. But just to play it safe, in case I had a problem, I asked a friend to write out the directions of how to get there.

He did.

But then, I paid little or no attention to the directions and promptly got lost. And I ended up miles away, at another school.

No problem, I thought, *I'll ask for directions.* But the school I had arrived at was closed. It was an official "skip day" and no-one was there. All of its buildings were closed and locked.

Now what?

I looked at my watch. Time was growing short. *I won't panic,* I told myself.

But I did.

There were no other buildings or houses close by, so, who could I ask for directions? Just then I saw a man trimming trees at the far end of one of the school's building. *I'll ask him. He will know.*

When I reached him I asked if he knew where the school was that I was trying to find.

He didn't know.

He also had no connection with the school where he was working, and was hired only as a tree surgeon to trim trees. "But," he said "Wait! I have maps in my truck. They will find the right school for you. Let's look?"

Then, sitting on a seat, half in and half out of his truck, with a book of maps on his lap, he began to search. Time was really going fast. I was growing nervous.

He couldn't find the correct map. "Be patient," he said. "We'll find it."

There was one thing I did know. The school I wanted was miles away, and my watch said I only had a few minutes to get there.

Then I heard something. It was the sound of someone walking. I looked up just as a man rounded the end of the building where I was. He was tall, handsome, athletic built, dressed in clean, neat clothing, and he was looking directly at me, and there a big smile on his face. There was no one else anywhere on the school grounds. Where did this man come from?

Then just as he was about to pass by, I stopped him and asked, "Do you know where the grade school is?"

He stopped and said, "Yes, and I can tell you where it is and how to get there." I was speechless Without hesitation, he began telling me about the school I was looking for and how to get there. And all the time he was doing this, the man in the truck was still searching through his book of maps. He didn't even know this other man was there.

I glanced at my watch, then I said to this stranger, "It's too late, my time is gone."

He smiled, nodded, then added, "You will just about make it."

He had to be kidding.

I looked back at the man in the truck. He was still searching his book of maps. He saw, heard, or knew nothing of what had just happened.

I turned back to the stranger to thank him, and he was not there. He was gone. Then, as I glanced around, I finally saw him again. He was walking at the far end of the building where I was standing. But there was something strange about his appearance. A soft glowing light flowed all around him and he was transparent. I could see right through him. Then suddenly, right before my eyes, he and that strange light disappeared completely. They just vanished!

Dazed, I turned to the man in the truck and said, "It's OK, I know where the school is now." He had a strange puzzled look on his face as if to say, "How do you know?"

I didn't wait to explain. My time was completely gone, but in my mind I told myself I should at least go to the school to explain and apologize for not being there. But, as I drove up to the school I was met with these words, "We were looking for you. You are right on time."

I couldn't answer or believe what I heard. I was speechless as I was ushered into the auditorium where the children were waiting. I was on right time.

Two questions still remain. One—how did that strange, young man know what school I was searching for? I never told him the name of the school. And two—how did I travel all those miles from the wrong school to get to the right one, and still be on time? My time was gone. How did this happen?

Don't ever ask me if I believe in angels.

You know I do!

A few years following this event, a friend told me she was there at the school that day. There had been several delays in the program until I arrived. Is this why that tall, young stranger said to me, when I said my time was gone "You will just about make it"? How did he know?

Chapter 4

How human was Ellen White? Was she some super-human being surrounded and protected from trouble? What about cherished wishes, wants, regrets, uncertainties? Did she have emotions, personal problems, secret desires, un-answered yearnings, or disappointments? Everyone feels pain, failure, even ridicule, and betrayal. What about unanswered questions or prayers, uncertainty, confusion, and feelings of worthlessness?

All of us know these things, but did she feel them too?

There are those who say she had an advantage over and beyond the rest of us, that God protected her from all these things. In other words, did she live in a cage, unaware of life around her, secure and above every human feeling and emotion?

Is this how it was? Did she have direct protective immunity from life's problems as a free gift from heaven?

How does one answer all of this? She told us herself in a letter to her friend, Dr. John Harvey Kellogg. The date was July 5, 1892: "I deeply regretted having crossed the broad waters [the Pacific Ocean]. Why was I not in America? Why, at such expense, was I in this country [Australia]? Time and again I could have buried my face in the bed quilts and had a good cry."

Does this sound like the reaction of a normal human being?

I say "Yes!"

So, how did she handle this situation? It was obvious she was discouraged when she wrote that letter. It was definitely a human reaction.

She answers this question herself in that same letter to Kellogg: "But I did not long indulge in the luxury of tears [so she did cry]. I said to myself, 'Ellen G. White, what do you mean? Have you not come to Australia because you felt that it was your duty to go where the conference judged it best for you to go? Has not this been your practice?' I said, 'Yes.' Then why do you feel almost forsaken, and discouraged? Is not this the enemy's work? I said, 'I believe it is.' I dried my tears as quickly as possible and said, 'It is enough; .... Live or die, I commit the keeping of my soul to Him who died for me.'"

Shouldn't we, you and I, not say the same?

The following is a section from a talk Ellen White gave at Pacific Union College in California. Her entire message was not recorded. However, the following passage was reported in *The Pacific Union Recorder* dated January 12, 1911 (Vol. 10, #24). This was nineteen years following her revealing letter to Dr. Kellogg in 1892 concerning her inmost thoughts and attitudes about her sickness.

"I have learned to trust Him in the past. Once for eleven months I never walked a step, and yet they said to me, 'we always see you smiling.' I could not move at all, except my right arm; but they made a form for my arm, and in this way I wrote 2,500 pages in Australia. I think I should acknowledge this here [at the college]. There are some present [today] who know how my strength began to recover. The first step I took an attendant burst out crying. They had to carry me to the congregation and carry me home six miles. But God works for us if we do our best. I have proved the Lord, and He has been true to me ...."

In 1902, Ellen White wrote to George Irwin. There is a sentence from it that reveals part of her outlook on life, especially concerning the close relationship she had with God. It reads as follows, "**Do your best, and God will expect no more.**"

Turning back to Australia again we find the question of where to live. Ellen felt a house would be best. But where was it going to be? It could not be just any house. No, she had a staff of workers to think of. Willie also needed to be close by, and what about her personal attendants? This required a place large enough for all.

She searched. They all searched. Several possibilities were found, but they were either too small, or too far away from church headquarters, not private or quiet enough, no fit space to do her writing, and who knows what else.

Ellen was not worried, however. She knew that when the right place showed itself, she would know it immediately. That had been the case all her life and here it was again. But God knew the need, and He always provided. She knew He would. The little house on Wood Street, in Battle Creek, Michigan, is one prime example. It was just the right place at just the right time for her, James, and their growing boys.

James and Ellen were quite a couple. Being married to James was like being tied to a tornado. And she was not far behind—a whirlwind herself with traveling, speaking appointments, constantly writing, housekeeping, and raising a family of boys. James was at the center of just about everything in the fast-growing Adventist church. He was a promoter, a born leader, president of the General Conference, and president of the Review and Herald Publishing Company. He had his hand in just about everything.

When he spoke, people jumped. He had the authority of a professional and others followed without question. Both he and Ellen had power. They also had determination. When James had a complete physical breakdown, doctors took over. Ellen overrode their decisions, and changed all that. Against their advice, she hauled James off to the wilds of Colorado, just the two of them against the wilderness. Their house was a tent, and it was so far away from civilization that it took pack horses to supply their needs. But he recovered.

Each had their own way of doing things. They went their separate ways, but were always together in purpose. There were ups and there were downs, ins and outs, triumph and failure, laughter and tears. These were two separate people emotionally, physically, and mentally, but operating as a unit of one.

Where these two in love? Of course they were. James' death in 1881 was devastating. Ellen fell apart. Her heart overflowed in a letter. She wrote, "I miss father [referring to James] more and more .... My life was so entwined or interwoven with my husband's that it is about impossible for me to be of any great account [value] without him."

Now she was in Australia, without James, and needing a house to live in. Was one ever found? Of course it was, but it took time to find it!

She made several moves, including rentals. Then when property was bought for a future school to be named Avondale (now a college), she bought part of the same land and began having a house built. She named it Sunnyside. Some thought the land was not suitable. It was swampy because of several running streams, but this did not stop Ellen. She just moved into a tent with all of her staff and waited for the house to be built.

Chapter 5

Let's talk about Australia, and as we do, we will also discover the who, why, and the what of the real Ellen White. Her thinking, emotions, decision making, relationships, and just about everything else a human encounters will appear. Some have believed this woman was not supposed to have problems as we do. That is because of who she was, and her close connection with hers and our Savoir. Not true! She had many of these trials and problems, if not more than the usual human has. Why can I say this? I'll tell you why. Ellen White was a woman in love, and she wanted the whole world to know. And it was Satan's aim to stop people from understanding this and her. Yes, hers was an active, ongoing love affair with God, the Creator of the universe.

In 1902 she said, "I shall be seventy-five years old the twenty-sixth of November; and yet … I feel … as if I could go to the ends of the earth, if only I could bring souls to a knowledge of the truth for this time."

Ellen White was over sixty-five years old when she was asked to go to Australia. She stayed there for ten years. And what did she find when she got there? She tells us.

"When we [her working staff of five] went to Australia, we found a little band of workers there, doing what they could; but they greatly needed help. We united with them in the work that they had begun, and during our stay in that country, about fifteen churches were raised up, and fifteen meetinghouses built; a school was established; and medical missionary work begun, small institutions being opened in several places."

This was a dynamo of a person. But of course she didn't do everything by herself to fill enormous needs. That was not possible. Her power-driven partnership with a working, devoted, God-serving staff made it successful. They worked together.

When she arrived in 1891 the church membership in all of Australia was 450. It went to 2,100 in 1900. 1902, and back in the United States, found her speaking at a camp meeting in Fresno, California. Sitting in the audience were several young workers who were about to become missionaries to the south seas and China. This triggered her memory.

Following the camp meeting, and thinking of Australia, she wrote, in a letter, "When I left Australia I really thought that I might be back in two years. [She wanted to return]. Should the Lord release me from my work in America, I know of no other place where I would rather be than in Cooranbong [Australia]."

For emphasis she repeated the words "No other place," only this time she added the words "on earth." Thus we read, "I know of no other place on earth so dear to me as Avondale, where we fought so many battles and gained so many victories." Ellen had all the reasons in the world for staying in the U. S., and for not going back as she wished to do. But she did stay in America.

Writing seemed to be her first priority. She was like a machine pouring out hand written pages by the thousands

This brings us to an investigation, a study, so to speak, of the true understanding and insight that made Ellen White who she was. So, what really happened in Australia?

Writing seemed to be her first priority. She was like a machine pouring out hand written pages by the thousands. Nothing stopped this. She was even disappointed she didn't create more pages when crossing the Pacific. Satan played an important role here. He was determined to bring this writing of hers to a complete stop. And he had a highly effective tool in mind for getting men, women, and children to reject God.

Three months after her arrival in Australia she was struck down with inflammatory rheumatism. She was almost helpless. Satan's plan was taking effect. From what I understand, with this disease, an infected person will suffer extreme pain in arms, hands, feet, and legs, as well as in their back. And a swelling of joints can often lead to deformity, and a fiery sensation in the throat, which can lead to feelings of hostility and anger. She experienced all of this and there was no letup.

What was her mental attitude? She wondered, "Why me Lord, why me?" Ellen had traveled for over a month, almost two, just to reach this isolated place because God wanted her to do it. There was so much work to be done, and only a few people to do it. The need was overwhelming, and now this ... she was a useless invalid.

Her thoughts are recorded. She said, "I do not understand why I am laying here." Then she reversed her thinking, "but God understands, and that is enough for me." Who of us, in that condition, could say such a thing?

This is the Ellen White I have come to know—the real Ellen White.

But while in this helpless condition, she made a startling discovery. Her right arm, from her elbow, down to and including her fingers, was not affected by this crippling, dangerous injury. As a result, a strong wooden cage was built to enclose that arm. This gave her, in a laying position, the ability to write, and write she did. Even then, in that awkward situation, she was in so much pain, that she felt she would not live to see the next morning.

Think back to Jesus on the night of His betrayal and arrest. He stated for all the world to hear that He could call, at any time, hundreds of thousands of angels to rescue Him. But He chose not to do it. Why? It was to save you and me, to give us a second chance at life with Him in eternity. He took our place, yours and mine, our penalty, and died a horrible death because He and His Father loved us that much.

Ellen White was doing everything in her power to do what God wanted her to do, and it was effective. Satan knew this. His plan was to put an end to her effectiveness. And he almost succeeded. Yet, even then, under such horrible conditions Ellen White continued to write. And what was it that she was writing that Satan tried so hard to stop?

It was a book.

The title was *The Desire of Ages*.

Her threatening, torturous illness enabled her to feel, in a very small way, what Jesus went through during His lifetime on earth, especially in the day He died. No one can describe what He suffered, but because of her own painful suffering, she turned to those days and tried to describe the agony He went through. I believe, as she wrote, that Jesus, Himself, was right there, beside her, writing every word she put on paper. He and she did it together for us.

As Ellen's condition grew worse, with no relief in sight, several ministers, and their wives, went to her home for an intensely strong prayer session. This was followed by an anointing service. Her immediate reaction was positive. "I have now done all that I can to follow the Bible directions," she wrote, "and I shall wait for the Lord to work, believing that in His good time He will heal me."

Notice the use of the word "believing."

In the meantime, the work of a growing church went on. But it didn't go on without her council. Meetings of church matters were held in her home, and she attended by being carried into the room and sitting in a rocking chair. As she eventually gained strength, she was asked to speak at church functions. On these occasions her son, Willie, and another man would make a seat by locking their hands together, sitting her on them, and then carry her to the speaker's platform and back again.

It was exhausting for all three.

This condition lasted for almost a year. "I have a longing desire to get well," she wrote, "that I may proclaim the truth in this country." She also added, "I try not to be anxious or to feel restless or dissatisfied."

She did recover.

And when she did so, there was no stopping her. She went everywhere … preaching, teaching, giving counsel, and writing. If a need arose, she was right there. And on her sixty-fifth birthday she said the best gift she received was her health and strength.

In a General Conference bulletin she reported, "We find no place where we can sit down and fold hands. Every town and village on the railway [the main means of travel in her day] is to have the message the Lord has given us. We can not stop to rejoice over a few victories."

Think, on top of all she suffered, she found time to write four new books beside tracts, manuscripts, letters, and magazine articles.

After nine years in Australia she returned to the United States. The year was 1900. She did not want to leave and said so. "To separate from it [Australia]," she wrote, "seems like tearing me to pieces ...."

But God was calling her back, and back she went.

Chapter 6

God and Ellen White had plans to create a college in Australia. Of course, the church was to back and approve the venture. This was a big project and it was met with a great deal of opposition. "NO!" some pounded on tables at meetings. "The church is in no position to afford such a thing. It is out of the question!"

Without recounting the battles that went on, and there were many, the final outcome was "Yes! With God's guiding, we will do it."

If you recall, we had a brief reference of this project in a former chapter. But now, we continue where we left off.

Land was bought … 1,450 acres of it. Many heads shook in disagreement. "The land is worthless," they shouted. "It is nothing but swamps and water, a wasteland!" But in spite of this, the land was purchased, and Ellen was delighted. So excited was she, that she bought forty acres of the land for herself. She would build a house. The price was $1,350.

Ellen did this for several reasons. One: she knew God chose the school site. Two: to show others she approved, and that it was the right place. She states this in her own words. "The reason," she wrote, "is that I may furnish money which they [the school] need so much just now."

The name for the college was, and still is, Avondale, and the location, Cooranbong. The year was 1897. But, one might ask, what would Ellen do with forty acres?

Remember, I called her a dynamo! Webster describes the word dynamo as an energetic, hardworking, forceful person.

Soon after buying her "Little Farm" of forty acres, Ellen White went into action. She bought tents, moved out of her rented house in Granville, and went to live on her land. The Granville house had been somewhat of a burden for her. It was like a free hotel. People came and went all the time. Most assumed she would take them in, and they were right, she did. But as a result, her writing suffered. This continued annoyance stressed her completely.

In a letter to Willie she asked this question. "But what can we do? We do not wish to say No, and yet the work of entertaining all who come is no light matter. Few understand or appreciate how taxing it can be..." She later regretted saying this. "I begrudge nothing," she wrote, "in the line of food or anything to make guests comfortable, ... and will entertain the children of God whenever it seems to be necessary .... God helping me, those who have embraced the truth and love God and keep His commandments shall not go hungry for food or naked for clothing if I know it."

The money for doing this, and other projects, came from her book royalties and from borrowing. Thus, tents went up on her new land, and the farm was her answer to the problem. She bought three large tents. This would be her home until a small—and she wanted it small—house, or cottage, as she sometimes called it, could be built.

One tent was for her, her granddaughter Ella, and a woman assistant. Another was for cooking and eating. The third was for the men workers on her "farm." Once settled she went to work clearing land. This was first. It was like a jungle.

Her son Willie gives a word picture of what kind of animal life lived on the 1,450 acre "jungle" plot, including the "little farm." This is what he wrote. "Of the wild animals on the place ... There is a small family of large kangaroos, which show themselves occasionally. The wallabies [a small or medium sized kangaroo, some the size of a rabbit] are quite numerous, although many have recently been shot .... The native bears are getting scarce. We seldom hear their cry. Opossums can be heard any night, although they have been thinned out by the hunters. Snakes are much talked about, but rarely seen. Each year we see less and less of them. Occasionally a tiger cat makes a raid on our fowls. Then we trap him, and he suffers the death penalty for his fowl murders. Flying foxes have done us no harm this year. Of magpies [a black and white gooselike bird], there are plenty. The laughing jackasses [a kingfisher bird with a loud laugh-like cry], though not numerous, are very sociable. Groups of cockatoos and parrots are occasionally seen. The bell bird and the whip bird can be heard every day."

Clearing land was a major job. It became top priority. "Log heaps," Ellen wrote, "are burning all around us ... Immense trees, the giants of the forest, lie cut up by the roots ... It takes days to cut out one big tree. We are indeed in the very midst of clearing and burning the greatest trees I ever saw."

So, what was she doing besides watching this activity? "Emily and I are driving a span of horses hither and thither." OK, so she knew how to handle horses and wagons. This was a woman who didn't know how to sit still and do nothing. It was just not in her make up to do such a thing.

Ellen had plans for her "little farm" and she wasted no time in getting started. Her plan was to leave some of the land in timber, forest, and some for grazing. She would buy cows for milk, and many acres more for orchards and gardens. Then, of course, there was a choice spot reserved for the house she wanted to have built.

She was a woman on the move. The year was 1895.

She made many seventy-five-mile trips to Granville. It wore her out, but she did it to obtain information from growers, about supplies, and trees for orchard planting. She and those with her—for she did not make these trips alone—also went shopping for camp needs for her farm. Cooking pots and pans were high on the list. Enamelware was also chosen because of its toughness.

Her first thoughts, however, were for her orchard. It was late in the season and she had to hurry because planting season was closing. "If," she thought, "I don't plant now, a whole year will be lost."

Her main "hither and thither" action included finding and visiting leading orchard growers in the area. They had vital information and she was determined to find out what it was and how they did it to be successful.

Here is an example of how she handled the planting of peach trees. The man who sold her the trees offered to show her how to plant them the right way. She replied, "Let me show you what the Lord showed me, in the night season, just how it should be done."

She then asked a man she had hired to dig a deep hole. When it was done, he was to put a layer of rich top soil into it. Next he was to add stones, followed by the tree itself and another layer of rich soil. This process was to be repeated until the hole was completely filled with the tree firmly imbedded. The expert tree planter smiled then remarked, "You need no lesson from me to teach you how to plant the trees."

The new school was also planting an orchard. As it was in progress, Ellen White's orchard was also being worked on. This became a friendly race between the two as to who would be first in completing the job. The school won by one day.

She was a real down-to-earth, red-blooded human being, not a do-nothing, see-nothing person. When something had to be done, she was right there on top of it

Ellen had a second, deeper reason for planting the correct way. The community was curiously watching the activity at both places, and she knew it. Here were her feelings as stated in a letter. "We shall experiment on this land, and if we make a success, others will follow our example .... When right methods of cultivation are adopted, there will be far less poverty than now exists. We intend to give the people practical lessons upon the improvement of the land, and thus induce them to cultivate their land, now lying idle. If we accomplish this, we shall have done good missionary work."

As I write these things about Ellen White, it is my purpose to present her as she truly was. Some people picture her as a person who sat writing or speaking, and that is all. They know nothing, or very little, about the other side to this woman, the one that has been hidden far too long. She was a real down-to-earth, red-blooded human being, not a do-nothing, see-nothing person. When something had to be done, she was right there on top of it. She was never afraid of hard work. It was her friend. Her practical feelings and concerns show in her dealing with the cows she bought for her "farm."

Let me explain.

From one of her letters she wrote, "I drive my own two-horse team, visit the lumber mills and order the lumber to save the time of the workers, and go out in search of our cows. I have purchased two good cows—that is, good for this locality.

"Almost everywhere ... they have a strange custom of confining the cows at milking time. They put her head in a fixture called a bail, then tie up one of her legs to a stake. It is a barbarous practice.

"I told those of whom I bought my cows that I should do no such thing, but leave the creatures free, and teach them to stand still. The owner looked at me in astonishment. 'You cannot do this, Mrs. White,' he said; 'They will not stand. No one thinks of doing it any other way."

I can almost picture her now as she, with a set look on her face, an unwavering, but determined smile on her lips, as she looked the man straight in the eyes, and said in a soft, gentle voice "I shall give you an example of what can be done."

Here we go again ... the true Ellen I know showing her colors.

We continue.

"I have not had a rope on the cows' legs, or had their heads put into a bail. One of my cows has run on the mountains till she was 3 years old, and was never milked before. The people have not the slightest idea that they can depart from their former practices, and train the dumb animals to better habits by painstaking effort. We have treated our cows gently, and they are perfectly docile. These cows had never had a mess of bran or any other prepared food. They get their living by grazing on the mountains, and the calf runs with the cows." She ended her letter with, "Such miserable customs! We are trying to teach better practices."

In the meantime, Willie located a well-known Adventist builder. He was from Tasmania, out of work, and looking for business in Sydney. When Ellen heard of this expert builder, she hired him for two dollars a day. He would build her house.

This woman was practical. When she saw that a job was needed, one that she could handle, she was right there. For instance, as work progressed on her house she ran errands for the workmen to save their time.

Even with all this activity, she found time to write.

Before closing this chapter, shall we look in on her in that makeshift camp she called home? She gives a description of how things were. The date was August 28, 1896.

"I am seated on the bed writing at half past 3:00 A. M. Have not slept since half past one o'clock. Ella May White and I are the sole occupants of a large, comfortable family tent. Close by is another good-sized tent, used as a dining room. We have a rude shanty for the kitchen, and a small five-by-five storeroom. Next is another tent, which accommodates three of my workmen. Next is a room enclosed but not furnished, for washing and workshop. This is now used as a bedroom by two men .... These five men we board. Several others are at work on the land who board themselves. Fanny Bolton occupies another tent, well fitted up with her organ and furniture. You see we have quite a village of tents."

Chapter 7

At this point in my writing I have come to what some might call a stalemate. I say this because of a question that has arisen. And that question is this. Should I include certain, shall we say, sensitive events that took place in this story ... or not? It is a hard decision, but it must be done.

> *If a human being is determined to do wrong, and knows it to be wrong, and does it anyway, in spite of His warning, will God honor that decision? I say "yes."*

At times God works in mysterious ways. He honors a person's right of choice. He will not interfere with decision making. He will, however, influence it. If a human being is determined to do wrong, and knows it to be wrong, and does it anyway, in spite of His warning, will God honor that decision? I say "yes." One example is Eve. God did not stop her from picking and eating from the forbidden tree. He told both Adam and Eve never to do this. His instruction also went with a warning. And that warning was vital for their continuation of life itself. Thus, He respected her decision, her action, when she made it. She failed to obey God's test of obedience. So, what did God do about it? He sadly stepped back and allowed the wrong to go forward. Although He let this happen, He didn't destroy either of them and start over. He never lets go of any of us until He has to.

It was Eve's choice, hers and Adam's decision to do wrong. The result, of course, is the fallen world we live in today.

Before Ellen White went to Australia, the church's headquarters in Battle Creek was in a state of deterioration. A number of officials were fighting for power. Struggles for top positions, such as finance control, plus political authority, were the main issues—all under the disguise of serving God.

They wanted complete control, and Ellen White was in the way. The solution to the situation was to remove her. In other words, "let's send her away, far away." Ellen was unaware of this. Yet she was confused and somewhat perplexed, wondering why she was asked to go so far away. She had questions.

Ever since she set sail for Australia she was mystified by this strange turn of events. She felt she was needed at Battle Creek and often asked the Lord a flood of questions as to why Australia. But His only reply was complete silence.

She was simply told by the General Conference that, "You are needed in Australia, and it is for an indefinite period of time." She did not want to go there and repeatedly said so. It was an isolated place, on the other side of the world, and far from the center of the church's headquarters.

But she went, and it took ages, as it seemed to her, for God to answer "why." And when it did come, she wrote the following: "That the people of Battle Creek should feel that they could have us leave at the time we did was the result of man's devising, and not the Lord's .... The Battle Creek matters have been laid before me at this great distance, and the load I have carried has been very heavy to bear.

"There was a great willingness to have us leave [America] that the Lord permitted this thing to take place. Those who were weary of the testimonies borne were left without the persons who bore them. Our separation from Battle Creek was to let men have their own will and way, which they thought superior to the way of the Lord...

"The Lord would have worked for Australia by other means, and a strong influence would have been held at Battle Creek, the great heart of the work. There we would have stood shoulder to shoulder, creating a healthful atmosphere to be felt in all our conferences.

"It was not the Lord who devised this matter. I could not get one ray of light to leave America. [This is referring to her not getting an answer from God about why she should make the Australian trip]. But when the Lord presented this matter to me as it really was, I opened my lips to no one, because I knew that no one would discern [understand] the matter in all its bearings [details]. When we left [Battle Creek], relief was felt by many, but not so by yourself [she was writing this to the president of the General Conference O. A. Olsen, who had not been involved with the conspiracy], and the Lord was displeased, for He had set us [to stay in Battle Creek] to stand at the wheels [center] of the moving machinery at Battle Creek."

Notice how Ellen wrote in as gentile a way as she could. The wrongdoers were still God's children even though they had gone wrong. Yet their actions could not be ignored. They had to be pointed out and exposed.

Elder Olsen urged Ellen White to return to Battle Creek. He did it several times. But every answer was **"No."** She did not want to go back. She had work to do in Australia, and beside this, she had fallen in love with the country, its people, and her new home— Sunnyside. She even enlarged her holdings from forty acres to sixty acres. And her little farm was producing and doing well.

March 7, 1900, she wrote, "I slept not. I was in conflict all night, pro and con. Reasons would urge themselves as though a voice was speaking to me, and I bringing up objections-why it seemed to me I could not go to America. And thus I reasoned and prayed, unwilling to admit that I must go, or that it was my duty to go, but the decision was not made."

But it was made. She would return to the United States. Even then she wrote in her diary, "I wish to go, and I wish to remain."

In May of 1900, she made known her deepest concerns, and her reason for not going. She wrote, "I dread everything like confusion. I have stood on the battlefield at Battle Creek. I tremble at the thought of repeating the experience." She continued, "We know they need help in America, but is it my duty to take this long journey?"

"The battlefield at Battle Creek!" Here we have it again. She knew all too well what was ahead of her if she went back, and she did not look forward to doing so. There were those in that place who were not convinced of her connection with Heaven, especially her testimonies and messages from God. It would be "a battlefield," as she called it, all over again. Was she up to it? She asked God for a sign. Should she really leave Australia?

Doesn't this sound like you and me at times? We fret and wonder, am I doing the right thing? She was no different than we are.

Her answer came, however, when she was far out to sea and on her way back to the United States. An angel appeared to her saying she was doing the right thing, and that God was pleased.

Try picturing this scene.

Ellen White was saying "good-bye" for the last time to her home in Australia. Deep inside her house, called Sunnyside, came the sound of footsteps. No one heard them, but they echoed from room to room and from wall to wall.

There she was, a small woman, wandering slowly about. She was dressed for travel, but she was in no hurry to leave. In some of the rooms she stopped and imagined the sound of typewriters, laughing children, the banging of pots and pans in the kitchen, and singing, oh yes, lots of singing.

But now all there was to hear were footsteps, her footsteps. No one was there, just her. It was hard, so very hard, for this little lady to leave because she knew she would not be coming back for two years or more, or maybe not at all. And in her mind she wished she could pack up that house and farm and take it with her. She had been so happy living within this place, really happy.

Her footsteps stopped at a large window. It is one she has looked through many times before. Her eyes were closed, but her lips were moving. She was talking with her friend, God. The words were just between the two of them.

When, at last, she reached the front door, she opened it, stopped, and turned for one last look. Finally, she slowly, very slowly, closed the door as a rush of warm air swept past, and she was standing on the outside. She knew someone else would live there, and it would not be her.

She carefully walked down the steps and toward a carriage. Those who were waiting said nothing. They just watched. Finally a small voice spoke. "Come on, Grandma," it said. "We're waiting for you."

The little lady glanced up, took one more look at the house. Then with a smile on her face said, "I'm ready! We can go now."

Ellen White was leaving Australia and she wanted to cry, but there were no tears as they drove away.

She loved Sunnyside. Yet that smile never left her face. For you see, Sunnyside, although she loved it, was not her real home. She knew that. No, her real home is in a place called heaven, and she could hardly wait to get there; but not just yet.

The carriage and wagons drove past orchards, shade trees, her son Willie's house, and lots of flowers. She just sat watching as she placed each scene inside her memory. She would never forget any one of them.

Chapter 8

Now, the big question facing Ellen was this: where would she live in the United States? She made it very clear that under no circumstances would she live in or around Battle Creek, or anywhere east of the Rocky Mountains. It had to be in California, near the Pacific Press.

As she sailed across the Pacific in 1900, she thought to herself, *have I done the right thing? Am I going where the Lord wants me to go?* This kind of thinking was nothing new for her. Ellen White's first thoughts in anything was always *God first, me second*. It was the set standard of her life.

An answer for her thinking came when God sent an angel to the ship telling her she did the right thing. She was needed in the United States. We know her thoughts on this matter because of what she wrote in the magazine called *The Review and Herald*.

Here is some of it.

"This was against my wishes; for I wanted to remain in Australia. I love the people there, and I loved my work. I have not lost my love for Australia, nor my interest in the workers there." She went on to add that if going to America was what God wanted her to do, then she would go, no matter what her feelings were. She always obeyed His leading.

> *She went on to add that if going to America was what God wanted her to do, then she would go, no matter what her feelings were. She always obeyed His leading*

However, the big question still remained, "Where am I going to live?"

A large house was needed for her staff of workers and herself. She was also thinking of Willie and his family. His personal support and energy was needed in her work. They should live close by.

After arriving at San Francisco, she crossed the bay to Oakland, and began looking for a house to rent. Everything was expensive. Most places were thirty dollars a month, and her income was only fifty dollars each month.

One week went by and still there was nothing she could afford.

So what did she do? She stopped looking. That's right! She did nothing but sit and wait. She even wrote about it in the *Review and Herald Magazine,* dated February 12, 1901. "I am done with house hunting." Then she added, "When the Lord provides a place for me, I will gladly accept it."

Here was Ellen White. She was almost seventy-three years old, extremely busy with meetings, speaking appointments, preaching, helping with plans for the work of the church, attending camp meetings, and writing. Her ocean voyage, hunting for a house, living out of suitcases, preaching, and writing was too much, and she was tired.

Willie worried about his mother and suggested a rest at a health resort near St. Helena. It was sixty miles north of Oakland. She liked the idea.

Thus, with a few friends, Ellen crossed San Francisco Bay on a ferryboat named the El Capitan for Oakland. In Oakland the group boarded a steam train going north.

And when they arrived at the St. Helena station, a horse-drawn stagecoach from the sanitarium was waiting. There was also a two-seated phaeton (a light four-wheeled carriage) for her. Friends were at the "San," as they called the St. Helena Sanitarium, to meet Ellen and her group. And what did they talk about the most? It was house hunting, of course.

Now, it was now God's turn to take over. And He must have smiled when Mrs. Ings said, "Below the hill [where the 'San' was located] there is a place that is just the thing for you,"

Of course Ellen, and the entire group, had to see it. And when she looked at it, she was so excited she had a hard time controlling herself. "This is a most beautiful location," she wrote. "The surroundings are lovely. Ornamental trees from various parts of the world, flowers, mostly roses of a large variety, an orchard containing a thousand prune trees which are bearing, another orchard nearer the house, and still another orchard of olive trees, are growing on the place."

Needless to say, I would be excited too, wouldn't you?

Work, meetings, and people to meet, were all waiting for her. Even her son James Edson was waiting to see his mother. He came from the eastern part of the United States just to visit her. And the General Conference president was even there. She was also scheduled to speak at a camp meeting in Napa.

She was really busy.

But all the time Ellen was doing these things, she was thinking about the house she saw. She even quietly disappeared from one of the meetings at the sanitarium to take a second look at "that house." She just knew her friend God had His hand in this.

And He did!

In time, and it was a short time at that, she was able to buy the place from the money she received for the sale of her house in Australia.

Look at what she bought!

There was 73.71 acres of land, a two story, seven-room house completely furnished with carpets, drapes, linens, dishes, and all the furniture. There was also a barn, a stable with four horse stalls and carriages, plus a hayloft to hold twenty or thirty tons of hay. There was also a cow barn with space for twenty-two cows. And that was not all—two carriages, two farm wagons, a two-seated express wagon, a double-seated covered buggy, two phaetons [light four-wheeled carriages], an old road cart, a hand cart, plows, harrows, hand tools, one cow, two horses and a few chickens were included. With closure, the final cost was $4,000.00 with interest at 6¼ percent.

Think about it! All this happened in little over a week from the time she stepped off the ship from Australia. God knew what He was doing. Remember, while on the ship to America, she wondered if she was doing the right thing? Then an angel came. He said there was a place all ready for her to move into. You see, when you let the Lord take control, He does things in a big way.

Never forget that!

Moving into this house was, as she stated, "like stepping out of my home in Cooranbong [Sunnyside] into a beautiful roomy one."

Did she give God the credit? Of course she did.

"I knew the Lord was granting me His rich blessing," she said. "I never anticipated so much in a home that meets my taste and my desires so perfectly." She also wrote in a letter that she was now convinced that the Lord definitely wanted her back in America.

> *God had much more work and writing for her to do*

God had much more work and writing for her to do. He was aware she was getting older and needed a quiet place for all His work to be done. And this, a house named Elmshaven, was the right answer. There, far away from the center of the church's headquarters, she could continue her work for the One she loved more than anything else—God.

All this little lady did, or ever wanted to do, was to serve, act, and be used in whatever way God asked of her. He wants you to do the same, your best. He asks for no more than that.

Should you, should I, should we do less?

Never!

The action, the thinking, the decision making of this one human being demonstrates what it takes to be in love with God. That was Ellen White. He came first over every emotion she possessed. Why would a normal, happy, and contented person drop everything and leave it behind, not knowing what lay ahead? That calls for faith. She knew there would be questions and enemies where she was going, especially from the Church she loved. People would try to stop her work. She was not naive. And she was no quitter either.

Above everything else I found from my study of this woman, there is one thing I learned, and that one thing I will never forget. I discovered that when Ellen was confused, perplexed, or in a tight spot, she would say to herself, *"It is all right because God is in control, He knows about it, and that is more than enough for me."*

She trusted God completely.

Remember, she did not know for certain that she was doing the right thing by leaving the United States for a far away, little known country. She asked for an answer, but God was silent on the issue. Yet from all appearances it was what He wanted her to do. Then after she arrived and lived in Australia, she didn't want to leave the place. This is, as I just mentioned, complete, blind faith in the God she could not see, touch, or even talk with as she could with other humans she knew and trusted.

Ellen was completely human. I refer to the discovery of Elmshaven. She only saw it once. Yet she was so taken by that one brief look, that she slipped away from her work for another look. She had a speaking appointment, yes, and friends from faraway places were waiting to see her. Yet, like a small child with a new toy, she was so excited she couldn't wait to get her hands on it.

Doesn't that sound like something you would do, like I would do, slip away, dare I say sneak off? Of course it does. She was real. She was a normal human being.

She was one with us.

Chapter 9

"NO!" Sara said. "You can't go."

And Sara was right.

The year was 1901, and Ellen White was in no condition to go anywhere.

But the General Conference session was to meet in Michigan on April 2 through the 23rd, and Ellen knew, just knew, she had to be there. She also felt that if she did go, to Battle Creek, it might cost her, her life. Physically, she was in very bad shape. And who was Sara that she could say "no" and mean it?

Sara McEnterfer was a graduate nurse from the Battle Creek Sanitarium, appointed to be Ellen White's nurse and traveling companion. And she was just doing her job by saying "No!"

Ellen's mind was in great shape however, and she felt God wanted her to make the trip. So, go she would, no matter what Sara or anyone else said.

Oh, there were continued arguments, from Sara and others, but they did no good. Her mind was set. And that was final! This was faith again on her part, a complete showing of trust and faith in God, but she did dread the trip.

There was one problem. The fastest way to reach Battle Creek was to travel through and over the Sierra and Rocky Mountains. That was a physical, and devastating, risk for Ellen. The altitudes would just about, if not, kill her. But, she said she would take the chance, as she had done many times before. Yet, as Sara pointed out, never in the hazardous, weakened condition she was in now.

The southern route was longer but lower in elevation. From Los Angeles it would go through Arizona, Texas, plus a number of other southern states, to New Orleans. Then it was on to Vicksburg,

Mississippi. From there it was an easy trip north to Michigan. This was quite a trip.

Four people would be going: son Willie, Sara, Maggie Hare, and Ellen. On March 7 they took the overnight "Owl" train from Oakland to Los Angeles. Fortunately the pastor from the Healdsburg church was on board. He gave them copies of the official and essential health certificates, required for travel through Texas, which he happened to be carrying with him.

Ellen rallied some by the time they reached Los Angeles and was able to speak to hundreds of people at the main Adventist church in that city. But it proved to be too much, and she suffered a relapse. She was unconscious for twelve hours. A doctor and nurse worked on her constantly until she regained consciousness.

Days later she began to rally. Although weakened, but able to function some, she was placed in first class on the Sunset Limited, a train bound for New Orleans. Two full bushels of fresh, sweet, oranges went with them. These proved to be very beneficial, especially to Ellen. They helped revive her. She and her party arrived several days later with only a few oranges left.

Satan was fighting her every mile of the way. It was his plan to stop her if he could. But God and Ellen had other ideas. And two bushels of fresh oranges helped.

At Vicksburg, Ellen White's son Edson was there to meet them. The long train ride seemed to act like medicine for Ellen; she was reviving.

She was overjoyed to see Edson and his family. It had been years. He immediately took her and the group to his boat the "Morning Star." Ellen knew all about this ship from his letters, but now she was actually going to see it. She was not only anxious, she was delighted, when she finally walked on it. This would be her home for the next few days.

The story of the Morning Star reads like a novel. I won't go into it here, but it is exciting. Edson helped build his two-paddle-wheeled ship for traveling the rivers in the deep south. His purpose was to bring the Gospel to black America, and former slaves, now free. The ship, 150 feet long and 45 feet wide, was like a floating town, with a well-equipped printing press and all.

After spending her few days aboard the ship, Ellen noted the tiny living space and working areas for her son and family, and for the workers living with them. She made this comment. "I saw nothing expensive or unnecessary .... Perhaps some would have been unwilling to live in such narrow quarters." Every inch of space was filled.

When she and her traveling group were ready to travel north she stated, "It [the Morning Star] has been the means of sowing the seeds of truth in many hearts, and many souls have first seen the light of truth while on this boat."

But the statement that thrilled and excited Edson, his family, and crew the most was this: "On it [the ship]," she said, "angel feet have trodden."

Chapter 10

It is a marvel, in her weakened condition, that whenever there was a stopping place on this trip, and Ellen White was asked to speak, she never refused. People poured out of towns, villages, and great cities by the thousands just to see and hear her. They hung on to every word she spoke. Many were there out of curiosity, others to learn and listen.

But what about the woman herself: Ellen White? What was her reaction to all this extra work, plus the stress?

Here was a sick woman pushing herself to the limit. Oh, yes, she was recovering, but slowly, ever so slowly. So why did she exert herself to do this extra activity? It clearly drained her vital energy.

At this point, in our story, we discover an important element, insight we might say, into the make-up, the life, of this unique human being. In other words, what made her tick? Why did she function the way she did? For without hesitation she accepted freely this extra time-consuming drain, especially on her health, without complaint?

She gives us the answer herself.

She avoided most private interviews or contacts. "I was obliged," she wrote, "to refuse to see many visitors, for private conversations [because they] were more taxing [stressful] to me than public speaking."

"As I stood," she continued, "before the people, I felt [or feel] that I was [am] leaning on a strong arm, which would support me. But when engaged in conversation with visitors, I had [have] not this sense of special strength."

In other words, she felt God taking over her entire being by speaking through her in public with His words and message. Truly, this was a woman deeply in love with God. "I was [am] compelled to save my strength for the times when I must stand before the thousands of people assembled ... "

With this in mind, she finally arrived in Battle Creek. And what was her reception? Was she welcome? Doctor Kellogg (John Harvey) opened his palatial home to her and her group. He also provided private transportation at her convenience. Nothing was left out for her comfort. But, what about the General Conference itself? Were its members happy to see her? It is hard to say, but she did have enemies and she knew it. Thus, the following comment, "Here my labors begin."

And they did.

It is not my purpose to record the happening of the General Conference meetings in 1901. No, the aim of this book is to present the woman, named Ellen White, as a human being and not a something, nor a someone, to hold up in awe. No, she lived, she functioned, she was a real person. And it is my purpose, my effort, to present her as such, a living, breathing member of the human family.

I will have references to the meeting of 1901 of course, but as I do so, the real picture of this special woman should emerge as one like us. She possessed emotions, bravery, triumphs, failures; a living, breathing person, as I said before, as you and I are.

Several unofficial, pre-meetings met before the official opening of that General Conference session. One happened on a Monday morning, then another later that same day, in the Battle Creek College (now Andrews University) library. Ellen was present for both. The first was held in Doctor Kellogg's home where many things were discussed, concerning the denomination's future wellbeing.

Arthur Daniells opened the afternoon meeting. The first thing he did was to ask Ellen White to speak to those present. She replied, "I prefer not to speak ... not because I have nothing to say. I have something to say."

Daniells strongly urged her to speak.

She finally said "Yes." She wasted no time in going to what was on her mind.

Instead of presenting details of what she said, I will make a brief summary. God wanted changes in His church and He conveyed them through Ellen White. The entire church membership, worldwide, was 75,000, and growing rapidly. But what was it that God wanted to tell the conference session through this woman?

One thing was clear, and she said it powerfully in that library meeting. She urged, stressed, that until they, the delegates, and the church at large, were ready to take the Bible and make it their food and drink, their complete life, He, God, cannot, will not, help or guide them. Only until they do and say as He wants and asks them to do, then act upon it, He cannot be with them.

A number of other things were also on her mind that day, and she stated them, but not to any great detail. That would come later. One thing, however, was to call for a reorganization of the entire church structure. What she was actually doing, at that meeting, was this: she was preparing the minds of these church leaders to set the pace for what was to come in the days ahead. Finally, to bring her message home to them, she made a strong plea by asking them not to quote or repeat, as some were doing, that, "Sister White said this, and Sister White said that, and Sister White said the other thing."

There was a pause in her presentation, and the room went silent. Finally, and looking directly at every one that room she said, "Ask, what saith the Lord God of Israel?" Then in a more subdued tone she urged that they, all, every one of them "do just what the Lord God of Israel does and what He says." That is the first order of business, private and otherwise.

If this woman were alive today, her words would be exactly the same. "Put God first, last, and always! Not continually quoting what Ellen White's words say."

The official General Conference session opened at nine o'clock the following morning. President G. A. Irwin was in charge. Those who had been in the library meeting the day before, now saw and heard in his opening remarks, some of what they had heard in that gathering. Following this, he officially resigned his position as president and formally called the session to order and it was open to anyone.

Ellen White stood, then walked forward to the speaker's platform, and was given permission to speak. After a few opening remarks, she then went right to the heart of her message. "Why," she asked "why I ask you, are men who have not brought self into subjection allowed to stand in important positions of truth and handle sacred things? ... You have no right to manage, unless you manage in God's order."

With deep compassion in her voice she called for a change. Emotion flowed from her every word as she stated things as they were happening in His church, just as God Himself saw them. Love sprang from every word she spoke. And those who sat listening to her went silent.

"Oh," she continued, "my very soul is drawn out in these things! Men who have not learned to submit themselves to the control and discipline of God are not competent to train the youth, to deal with human minds."

She paused, then added, "It is just as much an impossibility for them to do this work as it would be for them to make a world."

And she wasn't finished speaking yet. "That these men should stand in a sacred place, to be as the voice of God to the people, as we once believed the General Conference to be—that is past. What we want now is a reorganization. We want to begin at the foundation, and to build upon a different principle."

Her ending thoughts were, "There ought to be more than one or two or three men to consider the whole vast field. The work is great, and there is no one human mind that can plan for the work which needs to be done.

"God wants you to be converted .... There must be a renovation, a reorganization; a power and strength must be brought into the committees that are necessary."

The day before she was more pointed.

She stated then that the work of the church was controlled by a very few people who held top positions in the denomination. She did say the president was not involved. This was "kingly power" in the hands of a few, "control," she said, and it had to stop ... "Sharp deals," she termed, some of which had been made in the publishing houses. Money was involved in the name of the church. God knew and watched it all. He called for a change, now!

Needless to say, the conference meetings were thrown into a dilemma. Some were calling for caution. At this Ellen White objected by saying no one should block what was being proposed. After prayer and more discussion, pro and con, a vote was taken. The proposal of change was carried overwhelmingly, and the work went full speed ahead with changes being made in all directions. Larger committees were created, including representations from all phases of the work such as educational, medical, publishing, ministerial, mission work, etc. And it began with the top positions.

It had been a hard, long trip for Ellen White from Australia, to California, then travels through the southland of the United States, not mentioning her buying and selling of homes. At times she wondered if she would survive. She knew she must go to Battle Creek. She even had fears of her own, that she might even die in the attempt, but she made it; she was at the General Conference sessions. God saw to it. He was right there with her all the time, leading, guiding her every step, and every hard, long mile she traveled. He was beside her when she stood to her feet in that first meeting of the General Conference session. And when she opened her mouth to speak, He gave her the words to say. And every person in that meeting knew it. God was there.

This frail figure of a woman had fears, as we all do. But her fears were that she would not fail, but instead, do, act, and speak as her best friend God asked her to do, act, and be His spokesperson, regardless of the outcome. This was true love, deep, honest, devoted love, and it lasted for a lifetime.

This was Ellen White.

Chapter 11

With the General Conference session of 1901 fresh in mind, and with your permission, shall we leave the delegates to work things out for themselves? And, as history tells us, they did just that.

We will again dig deeper into our search for the real Ellen White.

Her life, and what she did with it, is not a made-up story. She actually was a member of the human race, and she did the things I have been writing about. But before going on, however, we need to discuss something else. It is a word, a word we all know. And that one word is "war."

> *Men, women, all human beings young and old will fight on the battlefields of right and wrong. And there is no promise by either side that the fighting will be easy*

War is usually classified as an armed conflict with two opposing sides. There are battles with each side claiming to be right. But there is also another kind of war that is just as deadly—the hidden war of the mind. Both have casualties.

Thus it is with Christians. Those who claim God as their way of life, those who follow Him completely, will always be fighting one battle after another with Satan and his followers. Those battles have no end until the final conflict with God being the victor.

What about God's individual soldiers? Will they stay firm, loyal, and faithful to Him? Or will some desert?

Men, women, all human beings young and old will fight on the battlefields of right and wrong. And there is no promise by either side that the fighting will be easy. Courage, faith, complete trust and belief in the leader of their choice is essential. This is vital. All must choose, and there is no exception.

Ellen White was one who chose to follow God in the battle for souls, and it was not easy, even for her. She fought bravely, but never alone, for she claimed God as her way of life. He was her partner and what she lived for. And, she was true to every word of her commitment to and for Him.

This is one reason why I write what I do about this woman. It is to demonstrate what can be done by just one fragile human being ... one who is completely in love with God and His Son Jesus.

You can do the same.

All of God's followers are not prophets, but there are countless others, just like her, who do as He asks.

Oh, but before we dig deeper into who Ellen White was, and why she acted as she did, let me add something that she said about herself.

"My personality," she wrote, "is not my own, and I have no right to use it for selfish purposes. I can stand before the throne of God and be perfectly clear on this point, for I have never used my personality selfishly. My husband used to tell me that I was more in danger of going to the other extreme."

And what does she mean by personality?

One dictionary states that personality is a visible collection of qualities, or the sum total of the physical, mental, emotional, and social activities of a person as it impresses others.

Now, before reading on, let's just stop right here for a moment.

You have been reading about a woman I never met. I have not seen nor talked with her. I also have little knowledge of what she looked like. Yes, there are a few old pictures of a woman dressed in black. She is usually sitting stiffly in a chair with a Bible in her hands, and there is a stern look on her face. But that is not the real Ellen White.

Some say it is. But that is not the woman I want you to see. People may scoff and make fun of this little lady. And, sorry to say, most of them belong to the same church organization she belonged to. I admit that everyone has a right to his or her own opinion. God will not take that right away from anyone.

But I have read. I have studied. I have researched. I have even written books for children and adults about this woman. And I have also known members of her family. Each of them, if they were still alive, would tell you, along with myself, that this woman stopped at nothing to give you God's straight message, just as He told it to her.

Satan tried to stop her. Oh, how he tried! But nothing, I repeat, nothing could stop or slow this woman down. She lived a complete lifelong adventure, involving devotion and love for God. She walked, she talked, she listened to and followed His leading, with every atom in her body.

If anyone has a problem with her work or her messages, as some do, let me just say this. Read, yes, I say read what she wrote; and I tell you, she wrote like a machine gun.

Just read; then criticize if you must. It is your right to do so. But there is one thing you should always consider. Know your facts before you make up your mind or speak. Ellen White was a woman like no other; yet she was a real live, breathing human being, and a woman deeply in love, as I have repeatedly written, with God.

After reading what I have written thus far, we will now change our course, so to speak, by going back through time to the 1800s.

And why will I do this?

I won't tell you why, because I want you to read on, and when you do read on, you will find a delightful friend, wife, mother, fearless adventurer, bold, and a normal, practical, loving member of the human family; one who was not afraid to say to God, "Here I am, use me!"

Let's see how He did just that in Texas.

Late winter 1879 found a covered wagon train of eight wagons, various other wagons, and light carriages rolling slowly across wide stretches of prairie land … a true wasteland.

The place, Texas. Over thirty-one men, woman, and children made up the group. A man, riding ahead on horseback, led the way. His name was James White. Ellen, his wife, was close behind.

When they first decided to go to Texas, this couple had not planned to travel in this way. But now, here they were, and it was rough going.

So, why were they doing it?

James, in California, was worn-out and stressed from his many functions of leadership in the Adventist church. Ellen, his wife, called for a change. His health, actually his life, was in danger. She convinced him that the warmer climate to the south was the answer. They could spend the winter there. He liked the idea and agreed with her.

As I mentioned, they did not plan on leading a covered wagon train. But this was James White. He never could sit back and just do nothing. He was a born leader and had to be in the main action, no matter what it was, or where it led. Thus, he became the wagon master for the entire trip.

Crossing the Red River was no problem. They located a place where flatboats were moored. These boats were operated by boatmen who, after loading their boats, used long poles which they pushed deep into the river bottom and shoved. This moved and guided the boat forward. Thus each wagon was floated to the far side of the river. That was no problem. But the far side of the river was.

> *"Drive off as fast as you can and don't stop or you will sink! DON"T STOP UNTIL YOU REACH SOLID GROUND!"*

The boatmen warned of quicksand.

As each boat reached the far shore, the boatmen called out. "Drive off as fast as you can and don't stop or you will sink! DON"T STOP UNTIL YOU REACH SOLID GROUND!"

They all made it.

Once they were safely across, Ellen White wrote, "We spread our oil cloth on the ground and ... sat down at our low table and took refreshments."

They knew they would soon enter Indian Territory. We call it Oklahoma today.

When they finally pitched camp, a wild storm overtook them and flooded everything. Ellen and three women slept sideways across a portable bed as water rushed beneath them. The following day found her scrubbing mud from clothing, bedding, and almost everything else, including pots and pans.

But wouldn't you know it? In spite of all this, she found time to write.

Then, from deep inside Indian Territory, she wrote that at night, "We have our wagons brought up in a circle, then our horses are placed within the circle. We have two men to watch. They are relieved every two hours .... We have less fear from Indians than from white men who employ the Indians to make a stampede among the horses and mules and ponies." These were cattle rustlers. Rattlesnakes, poisonous insects, and tarantulas were everywhere.

Even then, Ellen found more time to write and preach whenever and wherever she could. She spoke of a time when a large group of Indians were in her audience. She said they were very interested and attentive to what she said.

When the wagons reached Kansas they followed the Neosha River, and food became a problem. Half of the entire group was depending on her for meals. "No rest," she wrote "not a bit of it for poor Marian [one of the travelers]; we have worked like slaves. We cooked repeatedly [herself included] half the night. Marian, the entire night. ... Unpack, and pack, hurry, cook, set table, has been the order of the day."

Besides doing all this, she spoke, "every Sabbath to our camp ... and every Sabbath evening or Sunday in towns and villages."

Thus, she wrote, "We are on the way again, slowly making our way over the broad prairies of Kansas. At nine o'clock we turn out to let the horses feed on grass. At noon we all drew up upon the broad prairie to take our dinner .... Teams are now being prepared for another move, while Mary and I, Adelia and Etta [more of the group], are gathering up, washing the dishes, and putting the food in baskets. The order comes, 'Move on.'"

Was this long trip worth it, or was it a waste of time? Ellen wondered. Once, in Texas, two of the White's mules ran off. They were gone for days until a young man named Arthur found them. Years later this same Arthur and his wife, Mary, the one who helped Ellen with the cooking, were with her in Australia. They became close friends.

Later Arthur, whose last name was Daniells, became president of the General Conference in the United States for twenty-one years. It's strange how God works in bringing certain people together. We wonder sometimes, but it is all for a purpose, God's purpose.

We leave our wagon trip now for more studies about the real, live woman we know as Ellen White. After all, she was, as I have often stated, a human being.

Oh, yes, and by the way, as a footnote, that rugged covered wagon trip did James White a world of good. He recovered completely from his illness.

Chapter 12

Isaiah was right when he wrote his 58th chapter. He was writing about fasting, but it was much more than that. His words went deeper than what he stated. His was an explanation of how God wants His children to act … how they, we, should treat one another, friend, or, and even enemies.

The Living Bible (TLB) is clear on this. It uses today's language. It says, "I want you to share your food with the hungry and bring right into your own homes those who are helpless, poor, and destitute. Clothe those who are cold, and don't hide from relatives who need your help" (vs. 7).

There is a reason for my quoting these words.

In my research on Ellen White, I discovered a factor that is little known. In a publication titled *Spirit of Prophecy Emphasis Week For Seventh-Day Adventist Schools, 1966–7,* on page 36, Ella Hughes tells of her life in Australia when Ellen White lived there. The two of them became friends. One day Ella went to see Mrs. White and found Sara, Ellen White's nurse and traveling companion, hanging laundry to dry on an outdoor clothesline. She wrote about it. "Some of the clothes," she stated, "were the most patched I had ever seen. I asked, 'To whom do they belong?' She replied, 'Mother.' For that was what she called Sister White. I said. 'Why?' She said. 'Mother gives all the new ones away and patches the old ones, for she says the needy might not know how to patch.' Sister White always kept a supply of new dress goods on hand from which she would draw to help clothe people who were needy."

But not all of her clothes had patches, or were in such sad condition. She had much better ones in her closet, but not many. They were reserved for visitors, meetings, and her countless sermons and speaking appointments. The patched and worn out ones were saved for everyday activities and functions, such as gardening, which she loved to do.

This knowledge became clear when a visitor went to visit her in Australia. This is what she saw and heard. "She had on a black alpaca house dress which was frayed in the sleeves. She laughed and said, 'Excuse my rags, for Sara is too busy taking care of other people to look after me.'"

And Ellen did use the words "my rags."

What caused Ellen to say, "Sara was too busy," followed by "to look after me"? Sara's job, appointed by the General Conference, was to be Ellen White's nurse and traveling companion. So, why wasn't she doing her job? Ellen did need her help because of her long sessions with sickness, and her travels seemed endless. She was constantly on the move.

The answer is simple, and most of it comes from Ellen herself. At one place in my research Ellen said she had never seen such poverty and want as what she saw in Australia. This was heavy on her mind, and she determined herself to do something about it. This, as you can guess, is one reason for the 'rags' statement. She did without when others could benefit from what she had. She was also more than aware of Sara's skill in nursing.

She did without when others could benefit from what she had

As a result, when a case of great want came to her attention, Ellen did something about it. She sent Sara with money, food, clothing, or whatever was needed. If medical attention was the problem, then Sara was there with her skills. Thus Sara was doing two jobs at once: caring for 'Mother,' as she called Ellen White, and nursing the sick. She loved doing both, and she seemed to be everywhere all at once.

Here is an example.

Sara was asked to help a family where everyone was sick. The father had held out as long as he possibly could, then he too was down and lost his job. So, here was a family of five children, a mother, and father and all were desperately ill. The mother tried to earn some money by taking in washings. The only seating in the house was two old chairs, and the blankets for their beds were sacks sewn together—and it was winter. There was also no food in the house. Ellen sent food and other necessities to keep the family alive. Sara did the nursing.

In time, as the father became better, Ellen and her son, Willie, found work for the man at one dollar a day. As a result, he stopped smoking and in time, he and his wife both joined the Adventist church.

This was only one example of the many, inner workings of Ellen White.

My favorite picture of Ellen White has never been printed. It has never been taken by a camera, either. No artist has ever painted it. It is a picture that exists, or shall I say is found, only in one place, and one place only. And that place is in my mind.

Ellen White was slowing down because of age, and Elmshaven was the place she chose to do it. Hers had been a long, hard life; her story and the events of her years read like pages found only in fiction. But it was all true, every part of it, from the time she was born until the picture in my mind.

My next picture of her is not well known, and it happened at Elmshaven.

One dark, fog-covered morning, Ellen White awoke early. The air was cold, and the ground was wet, very wet, especially on the grass. But this morning was different from all other mornings because something had happened in the barn overnight. It was a something Ellen White was patiently waiting for. A new calf was born. She had wondered about it before going to bed. The answer was, "No, it hasn't happened yet."

But now upon waking up the next day, her thoughts were the same. And the answer this time was a decided, "Yes! It is here."

"I must see it right away," was her reaction.

But Sara had other thoughts. "No," she said, "You need your breakfast first."

Ellen sighed, but obeyed. Sara knew best. However, she was still going to the barn to see the new calf. But "Later" was Sara's answer, "The calf will wait."

Determination! Ellen had that, and now she turned it on. She knew how. Yet from force of habit it was well controlled by common sense. So, later it would be, but not forgotten.

Finally, with breakfast over, she pushed her chair back and said, "Now we can go."

"But it is still cool out there and damp. You could catch a cold."

"I'll wear my heavy clothes."

"You'll get your feet wet."

"I'll wear goulashes [boots]."

Sara finally gave in. Goulashes and warm clothing it was. And, in a short time, they were on their way to the barn.

The barn was cold. But there it lay, curled beside its mother on a pile of straw. Ellen was overjoyed. "It will be a fine cow," she said as she examined it from the tip of its wet nose to the very end of its stringy tail.

She loved it.

Next, she had to say hello to the horses. They saw her coming and began to move their feet and whinny. They loved her. She petted each one and caressed their fur, and she whispered soft words to every one. She and they had a language all their own. This was a happy time.

Then it was over and back to the house.

But as they were passing an old tree stump in the yard, Sara said, "Mother, I want you to sit here and wait because I have a surprise for you."

Ellen sat and wondered, *What now?*

Sara disappeared into the barn. And when she finally emerged, both of her arms were filled with tiny, newly born baby chickens. They were all small, round balls of soft yellow fur, and peeping. Sara laid them all on Ellen's lap.

Oh, what fun, what delight! Ellen had to touch and handle each and every one of them. And just at that very moment the sun appeared, bathing the scene with soft golden light as she caressed their velvety, fluffy bodies, and laughed. Holding some up to her face she, like a small girl, giggled. She was so happy, so very happy, as she loved each and every moving, peeping one of them.

And that is my prized and favorite picture of Ellen White, the one a camera has never taken ... one that no artist has ever painted.

Chapter 13

I am an artist and an author. These gifts, talents, require very little physical action. Most of my functions for accomplishment are mental.

But I have a very close and loved friend who just happens to be a doctor. **Lucky me!** And that is an understatement. Oh, and by the way, his first name somehow just happens to be the same as mine, "Paul." **Lucky him!**

Do I have an ego? Don't answer!

His ongoing advice to me is this: "Exercise." In other words, don't just sit most of the time, which I do in pursuit of my profession.

He also advised that I drink a lot of water.

I'm trying!

No! I am not big and fat, but I know his advice is right.

Years ago I decided not to live in a city atmosphere, and ever since then, I have made my home in country areas. At present I live high in the central mountains of Idaho. I have no, or shall I say, few, neighbors. I also live alone. People tell me that I am out of my mind to do such a thing. They may be right, but I don't think so.

I love to write, and this mountain, country atmosphere, is just right for what I do. I sometimes sit down to dash off something for a future project, and I tell myself it will only takes a few minutes to do so. But before I realize it, three or four hours have gone by and I am still writing up a storm. This type of action also raises havoc with my body, thus, I become exhausted from so much concentrated mind effort and work.

As a result, I have now listened to my friend, the doctor. So, during my bouts with computers and paint brushes, I drink water. And I often take time to haul rock and dirt from one part of my property with a wheelbarrow and fill in low areas or build up places that need it with that stuff. And the doctor is right. I feel energized and have far more stamina than I have had in who knows when. It works. I function better, both physically and mentally.

Now, you may ask, why am I writing this about myself in a book on Ellen White? Does being practical go along with common sense?

You know, from reading these pages, I live in a high mountain forest. Some of my winter heating, but not all of it, comes from a wood-burning stove. This means I need kindling to start fires. I could go out and buy the stuff, but that takes money (whatever that is). Therefore, I have made it a practice that whenever I am driving in my area and notice a downed tree branch, I stop, pick it up, and take it, or them, home for firewood.

Pine cones are also great fire starters. As a result of this action, I have more than enough kindling to last most winters. And yes, my own tree droppings add to the supply.

I find that most people never do this kind of thing. So why do I do it. Does this function mean that I'm a tightwad or a penny-pincher? (Don't answer that!)

I look at it this way. This procedure, or activity, does several things for me.

One: It fills a need.

Two: It demands exercise.

Three: It stimulates blood-flow, and freedom of movement.

Four: It does save money.

This woman was not only clever and resourceful, but she was also practical, and skillfully ingenious in her ways

To my surprise, Ellen White felt the same way, and it wasn't beneath her dignity to do the very same things as I have just mentioned.

This woman was not only clever and resourceful, but she was also practical, and skillfully ingenious in her ways.

Willie illustrates this from something he wrote. He was twelve years old when the event happened. The year was 1866. His father, James White, had been seriously ill the year before. He was partly paralyzed. Doctors analyzed his condition as overwork in mind and body, predicting he may never recover completely.

This is a long story involving much faith and constant prayer. It is one that I don't intend to discuss or review in detail at this writing except in passing.

He slowly began to recover. And as he did so, his doctors prescribed complete rest with no activity whatsoever.

Ellen did not agree.

So she took charge.

Willie and she created an exercise program for him, including outdoor activity in nature's fresh air. He made progress.

She tried to explain in her, shall we say, descriptive, and clever way, such things as the following. And they worked wonders.

This is what Willie reported.

She saw to it that a field was plowed for them, to make it ready for planting corn and beans. "Mother sent to town for three hoes. Father groaned at the thought." But James did unwillingly use one of the hoes because, as he thought, *How would it look to others if he just sat and did nothing while his son and wife did all that hard work?*

Male pride had taken over as Ellen smiled to herself. She knew what she was doing. Was this of benefit to James? We shall find out at the end of this second incident. It happened a few days following the first one, the buying of three hoes.

Willie reported, "One day as we were passing close to where large pine trees had recently been cut and taken to a near-by sawmill, Mother noticed a lot of large pine chips. 'Willie, stop' she said [the twelve-year-old was driving]. 'See those big pine chips. They will be good for the cook stove.' Then she climbed out of the carryall (horse-drawn buggy) and began to gather up the chips."

Now we come to the hidden reason for the stop.

"'Come James,' she called, "help me pick up these chips' [notice, she didn't ask Willie to help, but I imagine he did it anyway]. Regretfully he climbed down and helped to gather the chips. When the task was completed, [and now comes the hoped for result of her request] he was glad that he had helped."

And how did Ellen feel about this? Willie continues. "To Mother the two bushels of chips were worth a few cents, but the victory that Father had gained over inertia [inaction] was worth to her more than many dollars."

Does this remind you of her action in the Colorado story briefly stated at the end of chapter four? It does me. I didn't go into much detail then, with that story, and I won't do it now either. The story is too long. But the action on Ellen White's part is the same.

She went against the advice of the doctors of her day and took over. This is not saying we should do that very same thing today. No! I say never do that! Medical practice is far more advanced now than in her day. Doctors know what they are doing. But Ellen White was special. In the developing days of medicine, she had direct contact with the great physician, God Himself. We do not! The medical profession is far more advanced, and I believe God has been leading in the research and knowledge we are thankful for and count on now. Therefore, it is to our advantage for good health and wellbeing to respect our doctor friends.

She would say the same.

To stress my point, she depended heavily on doctors and their knowledge when she had ailments. Here is one such incident. In March 1911 she began a series of treatments at the St. Helena Sanitarium for suspected skin cancer.

Her comment about those treatments was, "For several weeks I took treatment with the x-ray for the black spot that was on my forehead. In all I took twenty-three treatments, and these succeeded in entirely removing the mark. For this I am very grateful."

But when thinking of one's all-over health, there is one factor to consider. Man has polluted the world's air supply. Cities seem to be the worst offender. Country air and getting away from the crowded city atmosphere is still the best counsel, both for one's health and safety as well.

Ellen White constantly stressed this point.

So now, I recall her thinking about buying three hoes instead of two. It worked then, and it can do the same today.

And, as I continue to live high in the mountains, I can happily look for, and pick up, fallen tree branches and feel good about it.

I will just have to start looking for more of them!

Chapter 14

Come with me in thought. There will be no need to close your eyes or make believe you can see what I am about to write. The written words will be enough.

The year is 1903 … the place, Elmshaven. Ellen White is writing.

She writes: "I now have a very pleasant room in which to do my work. It is light and airy. On the east side there is a large bay window, and on bright days I have an abundance of sunshine. The open fireplace in the room is a great comfort to me ….

"I look after my own fire entirely, at night covering the coals with ashes and in the morning building the fire and putting on a large log that has been brought up and left on the hearth. I get up at all hours of the night, sometimes at twelve, sometimes at one, and sometimes at eleven, and when I rise I build my fire and then sit down to write. Lately I have been sleeping till two and three o'clock.

"I go up and down the stairs as quickly as any member of my family, and do this many times each day. I feel very grateful to the Lord for providing this refuge for me."

She loved Elmshaven. In a letter to her son, Edson, she said, "You would enjoy the sight of the roses climbing up the side of the house, right to the windows of the second story. If I wished to pick some, all I should have to do would be to open my window and reach out my hand." Imagine the odor, the fragrance!

In 1902, she wrote a letter picturing one of her activities. It happened on a Sunday morning. Ellen, with a man she called Brother James, a person she hired from Australia to run her small working farm, along with two of his children, and Sara, made up the group. She said they "rode seven miles up Howell Mountain to get cherries—small black ones, which were given us for the picking. Several others besides us were picking from the trees. The platform wagon was drawn under the trees, and Sara and I stood up on the seat and in this way reached the cherries. I picked eight quarts. We took home a large box of the fruit." So you see, Sister White is not decrepit yet!

Doesn't that sound just like her?

But wait! Let me tell you something else.

Ellen White was stressed for most of her adult life. Some of it came because she was a mother who lost two cherished sons by death. And then there was the early death of her husband. That, by itself, would disable the mind of most people. Travel! Yes travel; she went everywhere and anyplace God asked her to go. But then, as you read on these pages, she had, shall we say, mental bouts, and I am putting it mildly because these encounters were actually battles, with the leaders of her church, the Seventh-day Adventist denomination which she loved dearly. Then, there was her constant writing.

She was like a machine when it came to that. Writing! Writing! Writing! There was no end to it. God demanded much from this little person, and she accepted it all willingly, everything He handed her to do. It wasn't because she felt she had to do it. No! It was because she wanted to. There is a difference here. She was deeply in love with God, and He always came first, no matter what it was.

But, and most people don't know this, and there are also some who do not want us to know about it, Ellen had a secret weapon. And what was that weapon, the one that pulled her through many tight spots in her life? It was none other than a positive attitude, plus a sense of humor. Oh, like the rest of us, she had down times, discouragements, worries, but they never lasted. Why?

Here is a story about that "Why."

A short time before her death at Elmshaven, Sara acted like Ellen's second self. She anticipated Ellen's every need and faithfully filled it as best as she could. And Mrs. White helped to make it easier by using her secret weapon.

Let me demonstrate! "As time went on, her [Ellen's] appetite waned. On one occasion as Sara was coaxing her to eat, her response showed that she had not lost her sense of humor [her secret weapon]:

'Well Sara,' she said, 'I would not want to die before my time by overeating.'"

Another demonstration of her humor is found near the end of the introduction to this book. It concerned that student from Pacific Union College and the lemon pie incident.

Humor! She had it, and she used it. This was one of her most effective and successful secret weapons. There were others too, but she kept them to herself.

But the use of that special quality—humor—in her nature pulled her through many tight, and sometimes amusing, places. It not only relaxed the mind of others, it also set them, and her, at ease.

This woman was definitely a human being. Even though she had a hard life at times, she stayed with it and not only enjoyed what came her way, but endured it as well to the very end.

I have a request. It is in the form of a question and it is pointed directly at you, the one who is reading these words. It is also extremely important that you take time and go slowly before you answer. Think carefully now, and be honest with yourself by erasing everything from your mind. Take all the time you need.

Here now is my question.

If God spoke directly to you, and you knew it was Him doing the speaking, and He asked you to do something for Him, what would you do? How would you answer Him?

He did that very thing to a young boy named Samuel. He did it to an Egyptian prince whose name was Moses. Others followed, and there were many of them. You know from reading your Bible how they answered. And none of them lived an easy life. God never promised that to David, Noah, Esther, Peter, John, or a man named Paul. And He doesn't promise it to you, either.

What would your answer be?

Could you do what He asks? It could cost the loss of that certain someone you love dearly, or everything you own. So, how would you answer?

Millions have answered it. They said "Yes."

Ellen White was one who did.

Enemies, oh yes, she—and all of them—had those. Satan saw to it.

God chose Ellen for a special work when she was just a child.

He knew her well even then. Satan knew her too, and began his own plans to stop her.

When she was nine years old, a girl about her age didn't like Ellen. And in a fit of rage she threw a rock at her. It hit Ellen on the head, and she almost died from the blow. Years later, when Ellen was in her late seventies, she made a short statement about that attack.

Here are her words. "Since the accident," she wrote, "that happened to me when I was 9 years old, I have seldom been perfectly free from pain."

Satan was effective. He tried stopping her, but his plan failed.

So, how did she survive through all her years? Don't be naive. You know the answer as well as I do; she was in love with God, and He loved her back. That made all the difference. He pulled her through that encounter with the rock and many others as well.

They were a team, God and Ellen, those two, a winning team. Yet there were scars.

At the time of her seventy-eighth birthday she was facing increasing opposition to her life's work, mostly centering around certain medical statements that she had written. This did not stop her, however, from doing what God asked her to do and write. She stood by what she had written. This also gave her an opportunity to make a powerful statement, which revealed her attitude and also her reason for living.

> *They were a team, God and Ellen, those two, a winning team. Yet there were scars*

Read carefully as she speaks, through her written words, the following. "I greatly desire that no contention or unbelief may cause me a single thought of retaliation against those who are opposing my work; for I cannot afford to spoil my peace of mind. I want to know that the Lord stands back of me, and that in Him I have a helper that no human being can exceed. Nothing is so precious to me as to know that Christ is my Saviour.

"I appreciate the truth, every jot of it, just as it has been given to me by the Holy Spirit for the last fifty years. I desire everyone to know that I stand on the same platform of truth that we have maintained for more than half a century. That is the testimony that I desire to bear on the day that I am 78 years of age ....

"I know where my help is .... I trust in Jesus Christ as my Redeemer, my Saviour, and through Him I shall be an overcomer."

Chapter 15

Tell me, what happens in your mind when I mention the name Ellen White? Does it trigger anything? Together we have briefly touched on different, shall I say, aspects, or sides, of this person's life. So now, what is your reaction?

Elmshaven was her last home. She loved it and considered it as a personal gift from God. And it was. Now, as we now look in on her once more, we discover yet another phase of this complex, God-loving woman's life.

Ellen was slowly fading in strength and health. Her mind, however, was as clear and sharp as ever. What then was her outlook, her attitude?

In 1912 Willie wrote the following about his mother to a family member: "If you were here this morning you would see Mother and Sara just starting out for a drive." He added that "Mother is gradually growing feeble, but keeps cheerful, and does not worry as I feared she would over the fact that she cannot write as much as in former days."

In 1913, Sara gives a further glimpse. She wrote to Willie, "Mother's health has been more than we dared to hope for during your absence. She sings in the night and she sings in the day (even while in the bathtub taking her treatment). She seems to enjoy her food very much, and I believe it is doing her good. We get her out to ride twice nearly every day."

And what about those rides? They were either in a horse drawn carriage or a farm wagon. The rides usually went past orchards, grape vineyards, and homes of neighboring farmers. At times she stopped to visit with housewives and children. She often learned that many of these people were in need of food or clothing and she provided these. Most were immigrants from Italy or France and came to think of her, for years afterward, as the little white-haired lady who always spoke so lovingly of Jesus.

In 1913, two years before her death, Ellen White had an important vision. It involved the St. Helena Sanitarium. The medical institution was doing well, but it was also operating on a limited financial budget. Money was scarce.

It was at this point in time when the institution's main surgeon, a man of eminent reputation, demanded more money, plus he asked for a percentage of the fees that were charged his patients. He also stated that if his demands were not met, he might, and probably would, resign. This man was an important asset to the Sanitarium and a Seventh-day Adventist as well. His loss would be a disaster. Many patients were not only depending on his expert skill and knowledge … they came to the institution because of his reputation. He was a valued asset.

This obviously threw the management board into a crisis. They could not afford to lose him. Yet they knew they could not meet his financial demands. Thus, they voted to ask Ellen White for advice.

After contacting Willie White for an appointment with his mother, a date was set. The meeting was to take place at Elmshaven. Willie also reminded the committee that his mother was old and fragile, and may not live much longer. Ellen White knew nothing about this arrangement. Willie was to inform her about the meeting earlier on the appointed day itself. The trouble was he overslept on the morning it was to happen.

When he realized the time had almost arrived for the meeting, he flew into action arriving at Elmshaven just a few minutes before the meeting. He told his mother all about it and that the men were now on their way.

Her answer was, "I don't want to see them." She said this mainly because she was not feeling well, and didn't feel strong enough to meet them.

Willie was in trouble now. He stressed the fact that the Sanitarium board was made up of very important men, including many conference presidents.

She repeated, "No, I do not want to see them."

Willie begged.

Finally she relented and consented to see the men in the downstairs parlor. She was unusually silent when they came together, and a stalemate occurred. No one knew what to say.

At last, after strong urging, she began to talk, and talk she did.

Her advice, from a vision she had concerning that very situation was this. Do not give in to this man, and she was very clear on this point. Do not give him the increased money he is asking for. She spoke with such authority and power that they all listened carefully.

She gave several pointed and significant reasons.

Here are some.

One: It would set a trend. Others would follow his example.

Two: It would cause strife and bitter feelings if others were refused an increase in wages. They would claim discrimination.

Three: Do not allow workers to control the situation or give in to their demands.

Four: Do not exceed the budget. If you do so, expenses will only increase until the institution will suffer great loss, or close down, completely.

Five: Remember, the Sanitarium belongs to God, not men, and an example must be set.

Other points were also stressed such as being consistent especially when dealing with the Lord's work.

At last when the final decision was made, it was unanimous. They voted not to comply with the surgeon's demand.

Before the meeting ended, Ellen gave the committee, and us, the following advice. "The Lord desires us to be consistent in everything. He desires us to follow the self-sacrificing example of Christ, and when we do that, His blessing rests upon us.

"Those who have the cause of God at heart must realize that they are not working for themselves or for the small wage they may receive, and that God can make the little they do receive go

> *At last, after strong urging, she began to talk, and talk she did*

farther than they may think it can. He will give them satisfaction and blessing as they go forward in self-sacrificing labor. And He will bless every one of us as we labor in the meekness of Christ."

The result was that the surgeon backed down with his demands and stayed on as a worker in the Sanitarium.

There was a second reason, besides her not feeling well, as to why she did not wish to speak to the group from the Sanitarium. These men, she felt, were appointed by God to do His work, so why were they not using their own common sense in making this decision? They were capable of doing so, but were wrongly influenced by threats from one man backed by greed from Satan. She felt therefore, that they should have, and could have, stood up to the situation logically and not waste God's or her time when they should have solved the problem themselves. They were more than capable of doing it.

And when it was finally settled, how did Ellen White feel about all of this? She wrote to her son, Edson "My work is not yet done; no, no…" It made her so happy. God was still working through and with her.

No, even at her advanced age, her work was not done.

But what about Ellen's writing … in her declining years, did she continue to work at it?

In 1912 she stated "What strength I have is given mostly to bringing out in book form what I have written in past years on the Old Testament history from the time of Solomon to the time of Christ … We are advancing as fast as possible.

"I have faithful and conscientious helpers, who are gathering together what I have written for the *Review* [*Review and Herald*], *Signs* [*Signs of the Times*], and *Watchman* [all magazines; some in serial form], and in manuscripts and letters, and arranging it in chapters for the book [her next project]. Sometimes I examine several chapters in a day, and at other times I can read but little because my eyes become weary and I am dizzy. The chapters that I have been reading recently are very precious."

Her attitude was positive. She wrote to her son James Edson: "Be of good courage ... The Lord is rich in resources. **Never write failure.**"

Willie wrote in 1913: "Mother's courage is good. She has no fear of the future. She expects to rest in the grave a little while before the Lord comes, but she has no dread. Her only anxiety is to use day by day what strength God gives her, in a way most acceptable to her Master."

In that same year, 1913, Ellen had a positive message for the General Conference in session. One section read, "When the Lord sets his hand to prepare the way before His ministers, it is their duty to follow where He directs. He will never forsake or leave in uncertainty those who follow His leading with full purpose of heart."

She then turned to older and retired workers. "God will watch over His tired and faithful standard bearers, night and day, until the time comes for them to lay off their armor. Let them be assured that they are under the protecting care of Him who never slumbers or sleeps; that they are watched over by unwavering sentinels. Knowing this, and realizing that they are abiding in Christ, they may rest trustfully in the providences of God."

She also focused on her last farewell address to the church leaders by adding, "When in the night season I am unable to sleep, I lift my heart in prayer to God, and He strengthens me and gives me the assurance that He is with His ministering servants in the home field and in distant lands. I am encouraged and blessed as I realize that the God of Israel is still guiding His people, and that He will continue to be with them, even to the end."

Afterthoughts

Sabbath, February 13, 1915, Ellen White, stepped outside her study, tripped, and fell in a hallway at Elmshaven. Her left leg was broken. It was downhill from then on until her death on July 16. She was eighty-seven years old.

Her death was extremely hard on Willie. Mother and son were strongly attached to one another. To visit her empty work room on the second floor was almost hopeless for him. He knew she wasn't there. The door was locked. But with great difficulty of heart he unlocked it and went in.

He wrote, "Everything was in perfect order, but the life of the place had gone .... The old couch and the tables and chairs and chests of drawers were in their usual place, and the big armchair with its swing board in front was where it used to be, between the big bay window and the fireplace, but the dear mother, whose presence had made this room the most precious place in all the world to me, was not there."

Of the many visual pictures of Ellen White, in my mind, one stands out. It shows her sitting under blankets before her fireplace in the evening as she watches its brilliant flames flicker and warm the room.

But my favorite portrait of her has never been painted. It is the one, as I described, in chapter 12. I ask your patience and indulgence for just a moment longer, because I just can't seem to control myself. I wish to repeat that word portrait of her so fixed in my mind that I feel I must describe it once more. It is so very beautiful. It is her.

If I close my eyes, I can almost see our little lady. She is wrapped in a warm coat, boots on her feet, and sitting on an old tree stump outside a barn. And on her lap are handfuls of tiny baby chickens all peeping and moving at the same time. She is smiling as carefully, lovingly she picks up every tiny ball of velvet-like fluff, one at a time, and tenderly brushes each one against her face. And just at that moment the sun, that had been hidden all morning, breaks through the clouds and bathes the entire scene with warm, soft, glowing rays of light. It was almost like a delicate halo of gold.

Never will I forget that picture.

When President Franklin Roosevelt died, two news reporters asked his wife, Eleanor, this question: "What can we expect from you in the future?"

She replied, "Gentlemen, the story is over."

But history tells us, the story was not over.

The living, breathing, Ellen White may not be with us in person today, but like Eleanor Roosevelt, the story is not over.

She was a great lady. And the ongoing legacy of her written words will remain.

No, the story is not over. It has only gained strength, for soon her God, your God, and mine, the Lord and Savior of us all, will be on His way.

And we can begin again.

Thus we close the story of the Ellen White I have come to know. She was a real human being, a warm-hearted woman, with intense feelings and compassionate for the distress of others. Here was a woman God loved deeply, and a woman who was completely committed and truly in love, with—**GOD HIMSELF.**

Bibliography

Unless stated in the text itself, the following are the main references I used as source material for the writing of this book.
—Paul B. Ricchiuti, New Meadows, Idaho

1. *Ellen G. White: The Australian Years, volume 4, 1891–1900*, by Arthur L. White. Published by the Review and Herald Publishing Association, Washington, D. C.

2. *Ellen G. White: The Early Elmshaven Years, volume 5, 1900–1905*, by Arthur L. White. Published by the Review and Herald Publishing Association, Washington, D. C.

3. *Ellen G. White: The Later Elmshaven Years, volume 6, 1905–1915*, by Arthur L. White. Published by the Review and Herald Publishing Association, Washington, D. C.

4. Spirit of Prophecy Emphasis Week for Seventh-day Adventist Schools. Topic for the 1966–67 school year: Ellen G. White—The Human Interest Story. Published by the Ellen G. White Estate, the General Conference of Seventh-day Adventists, September 1966.

5. Spirit of Prophecy Emphasis Week for Seventh-day Adventist Schools. Topic for the 1967–68 school year: Mrs. White and the World-wide Church. Published by the Ellen G. White Estate, the General Conference of Seventh-day Adventists, September 1967.

6. Spirit of Prophecy Emphasis Week for Seventh-day Adventist Schools. Topic for the 1974–75 school year: Mrs. White and Today. Published by the Ellen G. White Estate, the General Conference of Seventh-day Adventists, September 1974.

7. *The Advent Review and Sabbath Herald*, Battle Creek, Michigan, Tuesday, February 13, 1900, p. 1. Published by the Seventh-day Adventist Publishing Association, Battle Creek, MI.

www.ingramcontent.com/pod-product-compliance
Lightning Source LLC
Chambersburg PA
CBHW060554100426
42742CB00013B/2553